THE ADVENT OF *RESCUE*

2025 Advent Reflections
based on *The Rescue Project*

XXIX ACTS

THE ADVENT OF RESCUE

ACTS XXIX Copyright © 2025. All rights reserved.

No part of this publication may be reproduced, stored in a retrieval system, or transmitted in any form by any means—electronic, mechanical, photocopy, recording, or any other—without prior permission in writing from the publisher.

Cover Image: *Adele Pierce, "Hail Full of Grace"*
Daily Reflections: *Sister Teresa Harrell, Society of Mary*

✝ **lorraine cross** *media*
A MISSION OF ACTS XXIX

ISBN: 979–8–9897270–3–2
Library of Congress Control Number: 2025917102
Printed in the United States of America

actsxxix.org
lorrainecross.media
rescueproject.us

WHAT'S THE MISSION?

O God, in the covenant of your Christ you never cease to gather to yourself from all nations a people growing together in unity through the Spirit; grant, we pray, that your Church faithful to the mission entrusted to her may continually go forward with the human family and always be the leaven and the soul of human society, to renew it in Christ and transform it into the family of God. Through our Lord Jesus Christ, your Son, who lives and reigns with you in the unity of the Holy Spirit, God, for ever and ever.

I rediscovered this prayer somewhat recently after my annual retreat. I haven't been able to get it out of my head since. To my way of thinking it is the most concise and helpful presentation of the mission of the Church I have ever come across. And it is especially urgent, I would argue, these days.

Our era is increasingly being described as "the new great depression." Whereas the first great depression was economic, this new one is largely due to the mental health crisis, which is only beginning to get the attention it deserves. Anxiety, fear, loneliness, depression, and despair are on the rise. This is especially true among younger people, but it's hardly limited to just them. There are many causes of this struggle going on in the lives of so many people. Perhaps the root of the problem is that God has been pushed farther and farther "off the stage." When that happens, the human person made in His image and likeness loses all sense of meaning and purpose. If the human person is the only creature that God has willed for its own sake, as the Catholic Church teaches, then it follows that if we don't know who God is, we quite simply can never know who we are. Our very existence is a gift from Him – a gift that has a purpose, an end goal in mind. What is that purpose, that end goal? What is the mission of the Church? And what do these things have to do with the season of Advent we are about to begin?

That prayer at the top of the page gives us the answer to the first question: the purpose for which God made us was to share in His own divine life for all eternity, to be in friendship with Him and with each other. More colloquially, we could say God's purpose in creating us was for us to be His family.

If we were to offer the basic "arc" of the story of the Bible, that is to say, the basic arc of human history, it might go something like this: In the beginning, God, who is infinitely happy and not needing of anything, chose to create everything that exists simply out of His love, a universe that is beyond our ability to comprehend, some 90 billion light years across. For those of us who love numbers, that's 90 billion times 5.88 trillion miles across. In this massive universe, there is one creature in particular that is the apple of God's eye. The highlight of everything He made was and is the human person, male and female, made in His image and likeness, made to be loved and to love – in that order.

Tragically, however, at the very dawn of our existence, our first parents fell for the seductive lie of the enemy of our race, the devil. This creature – and he is just a creature – rebelled against God, a rebellion that was incited by his envy of the plan God has for us. Out of malice towards us, he tricked our first parents into believing the lie that God is not a good Father, that He cannot be trusted, and that we can be happier without Him. Our first parents fell for that deception in what is simply known as "the fall." And what a devastating fall it was! The result of our first parents falling for this deception was that they unknowingly sold themselves and us, their descendants, into slavery to powers that we can never defeat on our own. What powers? The power of Sin, the power of Death, and the power of the devil. Those first two are intentionally written in capital letters, for Scripture speaks about them as if they are governments that seek to impose their brutal and hateful will upon us. At a fundamental level, one of the most tragic consequences of the fall was that the family was fractured. The human race's relationship with God was broken; the relationship between men and women was broken; the relationship within man and woman was broken; our relationship with all of creation was broken. Ever since that tragic day, creation has been groaning, longing for the time when it would all be put back together.

The first eleven chapters of the Book of Genesis lay before our eyes in epic fashion how quickly everything spiraled out of control. When God, out of love, asks the man and woman what has happened, the man blames the woman. The woman blames the serpent. Brother kills brother. Hatred, murder, and a desire for vengeance spread like wildfire among those God had created for friendship with Himself and each other. It all reaches a disastrous point in Genesis 11 with the story of the Tower of Babel. There, humanity tries to make a name for itself over and against God, claiming they do not need Him anymore. Their pride results in the people being scattered, and they are no longer even able to communicate in a single language.

God, however, did not abandon His creation to decay. In the very next chapter, God chooses and calls a man named Abram and promises that in him all the nations of the world, scattered by their own doing, would be blessed. In other words, God promises that through Abram, soon to become Abraham, He is going to unite again all the peoples who have become divided, not only with each other but with Himself.

Decades go by and, against all odds, Abraham has a child. His descendants do indeed become numerous. With each generation the deep longing for unity, together with the promise that God is going to do something to put the human family back together, grows. And grows. And grows. In various and many ways God speaks through the prophets, foretelling that some mysterious figure is going to arise, a figure anointed by God Himself. This figure is going to be like us — the seed of the woman back in Eden. He is going to be given authority to govern with justice and truth. Among many other things, God promises that through this figure He is going to defeat and destroy the veil that veils all people, that is, the kingdom of Death, and also the kingdom of Sin. Through this anointed one, the family will be reunited with each other and with God. Strange and mysterious words are written about the one being born of a virgin, but what in the world could that really mean? Other strange words announced that the unification of the family of God will have something to do with a suffering servant, and that this servant will suffer not only for the people of Israel, that is, Abraham's direct descendants, but for all the nations of the earth, scattered so long before at Babel.

Suddenly, when the fullness of time had come, God sent a messenger, an angel, to a young girl in a small town in an out of the way place so seemingly unimportant it isn't even mentioned in the Old Testament. Surely, this longed for and promised one couldn't come from such humble beginnings?

The woman to whom the messenger appears responds to God's invitation with the greatest words ever uttered by a human being: "Behold, I am the handmaid of the Lord. Be it done to me according to your word." In other words, "God can do in and through me whatever He wants. I trust Him." And the woman's name was Mary.

And so, more wondrously than the writer named Shakespeare appearing as an actor in his own play Hamlet at The Globe Theater, the Author of history (His-story) steps onto the stage. The one who created a universe that is 90 billion light years across becomes man.

To do what? To put things back together. His life, death, and resurrection prove the enemy of our race wrong about God – He is a good Father and can be trusted. How does He prove this? By laying down His life for the creature He made. No greater love has someone than to lay down his life for his friends, and Jesus shows this love even to the point of a most humiliating and degrading fashion — the cross. By this death and resurrection, Jesus overcomes and defeats those powers — Death and Sin — that had harassed and oppressed us for so long. The one behind those powers, the devil, whom Jesus calls "the strong man," proves to be no match for the God-man one who is infinitely stronger. These powers are not yet destroyed, to be sure, but they have in fact been defeated, and no longer have dominion over us.

As we soak in this story, God reveals the remedy for the pandemic that is plaguing our modern world. The simple and yet life-changing truth of the Bible is this: You matter to God. God sees you. He hears your cries. He cares for you. He is not absent or distant. He wants you to know that you're worth fighting for.

You're worth dying for. To God!

Not just you, though. Or me. Us. All of us.

God's desire is to gather all of His children together. That's why Jesus died, John's Gospel tells us – not just for one nation but to gather together all the scattered children of God.

As we make our way through the New Testament, we see those scattered children represented in Jerusalem on the Day of Pentecost, where Genesis 11 and the Tower of Babel is "undone." Suddenly, by the power of the Spirit that once hovered over the waters at the dawn of creation, everyone can understand each other again, and what they understand is the apostles proclaiming the love of God made manifest in Jesus. Those very people return home to the lands from which they came, spreading the word of God's love, letting their neighbors know about the wondrous things that happened in Jerusalem on that Friday we now call "Good." Those first Christians, living in the midst of a fragmented and divided world, a world held hostage by the power of the Roman Empire and Caesar, not only proclaimed but manifested an entirely new way of being human, a new family that transcended ethnic and language and socio-economic boundaries. And people noticed. This new kind of family was attractive. It gave hope. It unified people that had previously distrusted and hated each other, that had once seen the other as "the enemy." Now, however, these men and women who had nothing in common were made one in their loyalty and allegiance to the God-man who had come to rescue them, and all of us, from the nightmare that is life apart from God. This new kind of human family turned the world upside down and forever changed human history.

When we finally get to the end of the Bible, what do we read? Surprisingly to many, we don't read us "escaping this world and going up"; we read God coming down, dwelling again with His people as He once did back at the start of the story – only somehow it's in an even more magnificent way.

In the end, He will be our God and we will be His people.

This is what the story is all about. This is why Jesus came. And this is the mission of the Church, a mission made increasingly more important because of the times we're living in and the situation of so many in our families, our neighborhoods, our schools, and our workplaces. God created us out of love. We were horrifically captured by a creature who hates us and wants to destroy us. But God Himself in a most creative and stunning way rescued us from this creature, and from all his malicious schemes. And now our response is to praise and thank and glorify the God who has done this.

The response, though, is not just to praise and thank and glorify God. It's also to tell those who do not know they matter to God the great and good news of what He has done for us, to give them hope. It's to let them know they are beloved sons and daughters of God, that He cares for them, that He sees their hurts, that He has borne their grief and pain, and that He is able to make all things new.

The response is also to be active and living agents and instruments in God's hands, seeking to implement the love, truth, and beauty of the Kingdom of God, seeking to let the power of the Gospel touch and transform – like leaven in dough – everything it touches, until the Lord Jesus returns in glory and there is a new heaven and a new earth.

Our mission as the Church is to walk with this lonely, divided, anxious, and fearful human family; to give them hope, a hope that is rooted in the concrete and historical action of God; to announce that it is possible to be transformed, to start again, to be reconciled with God and with each other – no matter what; and to transform the human family into the family of God.

This is the story into which you and I have been born. And nothing is more life-giving, more dramatic, more worthwhile, more heroic, more epic, than playing our part.

FR. JOHN RICCARDO

JUNE 29, 2025

INTRODUCTION

The first Advent, in the Holy Land, only Mary and Joseph were watching for the coming of the Lord Jesus Christ. They were eager for His coming, awaiting His birth with great love and longing, joyfully expecting him to come any moment, any day.

And it wasn't that their waiting was easy. In fact, it was a difficult waiting, because, in her third trimester, Mary and Joseph had to pick up and leave their humble home in Nazareth, and travel ninety miles to Bethlehem, all because of a census tax imposed by occupying Roman forces. Nonetheless, even though the journey was difficult, each day they waited for Jesus to come with great love and longing, trusting that God had a reason for the struggles as they waited for the Christ child to be born.

In many ways, our world is not so different from the world into which Christ was born some 2000+ years ago. There are wars and conflicts, nations imposing themselves upon weaker nations, injustice, poverty, hardship. There are people immigrating, legally and illegally, fleeing oppression and danger, or looking for a better life. And, like in the days of Mary and Joseph, most of the world seems indifferent to and ignorant of this season of Advent, this season of expectation, this season filled with the promise and the hope of the coming of the Lord Jesus Christ. Perhaps in your family, you are the only one watching. Perhaps you know others who are expecting, but with fear. Perhaps even in your faith community, this season is largely forgotten with all the Christmas festivities and shopping.

But even were you watching alone in your family or in your friend group or in your community, you never watch alone.

Advent is a season that the whole Church takes up, longing for the coming of Her Lord. Advent is a season in which Mary and Joseph are particularly present, accompanying us, teaching us to long for and look for and prepare our hearts for Jesus to come.

Because he will come. He who came 2000+ years ago will come again this Christmas, as He will come again at the end of the age. And to prepare our hearts for His coming, to prepare room for him, to increase our desire for him, to open more space in our lives for him, we invite you to join us in meditating on the Scriptures, to understand anew and more deeply just what Jesus' coming into this world means, for the world itself, and for each one of us.

These meditations will follow the kerygma, the essential proclamation of the Gospel: God created this world—and each one of us—good and beautiful, in the abundance of His love; this world and each one of us was captured by a powerful—yet created—Enemy from whom we cannot free ourselves; out of tremendous mercy, God himself became incarnate in Jesus Christ, who rescued us from slavery and gives us a new life; because Jesus has saved us, we can choose to respond with love and generosity, living that new life more and more fully.

Some Tips For Prayer

It's helpful to prepare a place for your prayer, if you are not praying in a chapel or church before the Blessed Sacrament. Try to have the same place every day, a kind of permanent "prayer corner" in your room or in your home, with a small "altar" where you have a crucifix or image of Jesus, an image of Our Lady, a candle, and your Bible. Invoke the Holy Spirit to begin your time of prayer. The same Holy Spirit who inspired the writing of each word of the Bible wants to come to you and open up the Scriptures to you, but He always waits for the invitation. So spend some time invoking the Holy Spirit, asking Him to open the Scriptures to you and open you to the Scriptures.

Pray the Advent prayer that follows below.

Slowly read the daily readings in your own Bible, and spend a few moments pondering them.

Advent Prayer

Jesus, I want to be ready for You to come. Not just at the end of time, whenever that may be, but right here, right now, in my life today. I want to receive You. I want to watch for You.

Help me to set aside all distractions. Help me not to let the difficulties or challenges, joys or blessings of my life right now take my heart away from You; I want to stay focused on You. You are coming to redeem me, to rescue me, to give me new life. Let me look for You each day and at each moment, and especially now, as I pray with Your word. Mary and Joseph, I ask you to journey with me this Advent, to teach me to live in humble and joyful expectation even in the midst of difficulties and hardships. Teach me, like you, to be attentive to every small movement of Jesus' new life within me. Teach me, like you, to receive Jesus in God's word today, and to nurture and nourish and provide for that word, so that it can grow in me and be born in my actions.

SR. TERESA HARRELL
ADVENT 2025

week one
CREATED

In this first week of Advent, the Lord God invites us to reflect on the beautiful reality that we have been created by Him, out of the abundance of His love for us. The truths entailed in being creatures, being created in the image and likeness of God are so many, so rich, so beautiful, and returning to this reality, that we are created, will help us know both who God is and who we are, and thus how to live.

Sunday, November 30

Isaiah 2:1–5
Romans 13:11–14
Matthew 24:37–44

"Stay awake"

When heaven is described in the book of Revelation, it says there will be no night there, because we will be in the presence of God, who is light, so eternity will be a kind of endless day. Though there was night here on earth from the beginning, and human bodies need sleep and rest, our inattentiveness is not part of our nature; it's a result of the Fall.

In the beginning, we were awake, always awake, not necessarily physically, but emotionally, intellectually, spiritually. We were filled with awe and wonder at the beauty of creation, and the wonder of our own being, at the continual and loving presence of our God. Adam and Eve were attentive to the evening breeze, because they knew that somehow it signaled a daily encounter with God, who would come to "walk with them" in the Garden. They were attentive to each other, aware of the other's need and desires, gifts and talents.

They looked closely at the creatures that shared the garden with them, learning their natures, and could have described with perfection each fruit from the trees, each vegetable from the earth. They were attentive to the passing of days and seasons, watching how things grew, cultivating the garden with care and love and delight.

They were fully awake. Their senses didn't dim their intellect; their desires didn't overshadow their knowledge; their healthy love for their own lives didn't compete with their love for the other or for God. They were awake. They watched for the signs of God's presence in each moment, paid attention to one another, knew the animals by name. And it wasn't tiring for them; it was thrilling, life-giving, joyous.

They were awake the way you and I are in moments of awe-filled wonder: when we see the Northern lights dance across the night sky, or when we look up at the sky from somewhere in the country and see billions of stars in one glance, or when we hold a newborn baby, or when we are expecting someone we love to arrive from a journey.

That's how we were created to live: in joyful expectation, knowing each moment, each thing, each person is a gift to be cherished, a revelation of God's love, expecting a revelation from everything and everyone, attentive and delighted in the true deep-down goodness of everything and everyone.

Today Jesus invites us to wake up, to live this Advent in hopeful expectation, to pay attention today and each day to all the marvelous manifestations of the goodness of each person, each thing, each moment.

Questions for reflection

1. How awake are you to yourself, to others, to the world around you, to the presence of God? How can you cultivate that spirit of being awake?

2. What are the things (habits, desires, sins, etc.) that make you spiritually or emotionally drowsy? What step can you take to overcome them and choose instead to be awake?

3. When was the last time you closely observed or attended to something and let yourself be moved by the wonder of it all?

> ### Action
> Today choose not to multi-task, and instead focus on one thing at a time. In particular, choose to attend to each person who speaks with you, closing your computer, turning off your phone, etc., so that you can be awake and focused on that person and his or her goodness.

Homily Preaching
RESOURCES

Sunday Homily Resources

Advent will conclude, of course, with the Solemnity of the birth of the Lord Jesus. However, there's often not a lot of clarity on the reason why the eternal Son of God became flesh, born of the Virgin Mary. What exactly was the mission of Jesus? The Sundays of Advent are a wonderful opportunity to help a parish better understand Jesus' mission, and to bring everyone along on a sort of extended retreat in preparation for Christmas. What is offered below is a suggestion for how a priest or deacon may choose to preach the kerygma in these holy weeks with this goal in mind. The suggestions are based on *The Rescue Project*, which we strongly recommend parishes consult as they move through Advent (rescueproject.us). Each week breaks open one of four "big questions" that lie at the heart of *The Rescue Project* , and be helpful in understanding both the story of salvation history in general and the kerygma in particular:

1. Why is there something rather than nothing?
2. Why is everything so obviously messed up?
3. What, if anything, has God done about it? And
4. How should I respond?

These four "big questions" can be simplified to four words:
1. Created
2. Captured
3. Rescued
4. Response

Summary Points from Rescued
Part I: Created
Asking God for the graces of wonder and trust.

Key Truths

- ⚜ Genesis is unique among creation accounts.

- ⚜ Matter is good.

- ⚜ God created out of love, not need.

- ⚜ Humanity is the crown of creation, male and female he created them. The first blessing is the marital act: unitive and procreative.

- ⚜ We want the faithful to be filled with wonder and awe at the beauty of creation and how beauty reveals God.

- ⚜ "Created" is not really about proofs for God but *why* God created – love for humanity and for each one of us as well as the beauty and grandeur of creation and what it reveals about God and his power.

May we all be overwhelmed in the days ahead by what the Lord has done for us! May we be moved by the Holy Spirit to surrender ourselves more fully to God! And may we be mobilized for mission to go and evangelize and recreate this world that He sent His only Son.

Consider

To begin with creation is to ponder the question, "Why is there something instead of nothing?" Science can tell us how the universe has unfolded, but it cannot tell us why it exists. Revelation is how God shows us the answer to that question.

More than presenting proofs for the existence of God, this message is really about why God created: out of love. "In the beginning, God created..." Why? Not out of need, in the Trinity, He is complete; He has no need to create. He simply wanted us to be. All of creation, in its incredible magnitude, displays the power and love of God in a way that should make us wonder and be still, in awe at the God who created it.

All of it, however, is ultimately about us. Anything exists at all because God wanted us to exist, because He loves us. Humanity is the pinnacle of God's creation. "The first in intention is the last in execution," and God only rests in Genesis after creating humanity. This reveals to us the grandeur of our human nature and shows what we are made for – to be loved by and love God and from that love to move into relationship with one another. The original holiness leads to original unity – in John Paul's phraseology from the Theology of the Body addresses.

God's creative love in this way is not general but specific. He created everything because he loves, not just humanity, generally, but me, personally. His creative act is constant because He is the "ground of all being" (Aquinas) meaning He is constantly holding us in being by His creative love, constantly willing us and choosing us. "Each of us is the result of a thought of God. Each of us is willed. Each of us is loved. Each of us is necessary." (Pope Benedict XVI)

Possible Verses for Focus

Isaiah 2:2–3 – "All nations shall stream toward it; many peoples shall come and say: "Come, let us climb the Lord's mountain, to the house of the God of Jacob, that he may instruct us in his ways, and we may walk in his paths." We are compelled to seek God; we have a deep desire to know why we exist and what our purpose in life may be. These are invitations to faith in understanding the reason for creation, specifically our individual creation. This desire is a shared human experience that reflects the imprint on our hearts from our creator.

Psalm 22:1–9 – We were created for joy. God wants to bless us with his love and the life we've been given. Jerusalem was home to the temple, there was great rejoicing in believers that experienced the encounter with God at the temple. We're also reminded that God desires our peace and prosperity – we were made for good … and to have good relationships with God and others.

Matthew 24:44 – "So too, you also must be prepared, for at an hour you do not expect, the Son of Man will come." What does it mean to be prepared? How might Jesus be asking us to prepare? We can begin to prepare by taking the time to listen and learn; to accept this invitation into a deeper contemplation of our faith. Why does any of this matter? Why does life matter? Creating time to think about these big questions will help us better understand what preparation must take place.

Monday, December 1

Isaiah 2:1–5; Matthew 8:5–11

"I am not worthy"

"The centurion in today's Gospel has it right. Who of us is worthy that the Lord God, Creator of heaven and earth, enter under our roof? That's why we say this phrase each Mass, before receiving Jesus Himself in holy communion.

When we are in the presence of God, when we realize that God is God and we are not, when we remember that we are made from the dust, this is our response, too. It's not a self-negating, self-hating response, but a response of humility, which in both Latin and Greek has the same root as humus, earth. When God created Adam in the beginning, God created him from the dust of the earth, and this awareness of our smallness, our finiteness, our createdness, is essential for true humility. You and I, we are so, so small. On this planet, we occupy just a tiny bit of space. In this universe, 93+ billion light years across, we are seemingly infinitesimally unimportant. And in history, we are here for some 70–80 years, perhaps, of the 13.7 billion years of the universe. And this awareness of our smallness is an essential aspect of humility.

But it is not the whole of humility. Humility doesn't mean only seeing our smallness, but also seeing our worth in the eyes of our Creator. Scripture tells us that God knew us before forming us in the womb, that we are fearfully and wonderfully made, that we are one of a kind, unrepeatable, precious in the eyes of God.

True humility is a recognition both of our smallness and of our value, both of what we cannot do and what we can do. True humility means acknowledging who we are in the eyes of God and how God has gifted us individually. Some of the great Jewish rabbis have taught that the Hebrew word for humility, anavah, means to occupy one's unique place in the world, which implies accepting both our limits and our gifts, and living to the fullest, filling our own unique place in the world to the fullest.

Today let's ask for the grace of this humility: to see ourselves as God sees us, to acknowledge and receive and give back the gifts He has given us, to be aware of our smallness and dependence on Him, and to fill the space where He has placed us as no one else can.

Questions for reflection

1. How easy is it for you to recognize your smallness, your dependence on God? What step do you need to take here? How do you see your own worth?

2. What place in the world has God given you to occupy? How does He call you to occupy that place?

3. How often do you praise God for having created you just as He has created you? Why?

Action

Today spend 10 minutes in prayer of praise to God, both for your limits, which open you to others' gifts, and for your gifts.

Tuesday, December 2

ISAIAH 11:1–10; LUKE 10:21–24

"The earth shall be filled with the knowledge of the Lord"

The sun is slowly lowering itself into the Pacific Ocean, passing behind layers of clouds that it lights up from behind, spreading rays of yellow and pink light above and below. Wave after wave crashes onto the sand. Seagulls cry out. The sky shifts from blue to silver to orange to pink, the ocean from blue to gray, to milky silver. The waves crash ceaselessly. It is a glorious sunset, a beauty that catches at your breath, that lifts your heart.

St. Paul writes in Romans that we are without excuse if we don't recognize God from His creation, because creation manifests the invisible aspects of God. The ocean is powerful and constant, deeper than we can fathom, full of more life than we can guess at. The grains of sand on this beach in front of me are innumerable—we have no way of counting them all. And this is just one stretch of beach along one coastline of one ocean.

In the beginning, the whole earth was filled with the knowledge of the Lord. Nothing darkened our understanding. Nothing blinded us from seeing him present in his creation, from recognizing that everything we have ever seen or heard or smelled or touched or tasted in nature comes from his creating hand. Everything spoke to us of God, because everything was spoken into existence by the Word of God.

Sometimes I think we have silenced creation—but that's inaccurate. We have rather deafened ourself to it, filling our ears with so many other voices and sounds that it's hard to quiet our minds and hearts long enough to let things speak again.

We need to learn again to listen. We need to go to the ocean beaches, or stand on the shore of the lake, or climb a mountain, or hike a waterfall, or take a walk in the woods, or even just step outside, into our own yard, and marvel. This ocean! This river! This tree! This budding flower! All of it so precious in detail, each thing a word from God, telling us something about Him.

Adam and Eve, in the garden, must have delighted in discovering each day something new about God as they discovered some new thing, examining it, not to dissect it and break it into parts and control it, but to know it and understand it and love it, and through it to know and understand and love God the more. And we can do the same.

The earth is full of the knowledge of the Lord. We just need to let ourselves be taught again, to take the time to stop and look and listen and touch. Things will tell us, and like Adam and Eve, we can discover each day something more about God by listening to the things that he has made.

Questions for reflection

1. Where in nature is it easiest for you to contemplate God through creation? Why?

2. What have you learned when you have let things in this world speak to you, tell you what they are and what they have to say about God?

3. What are the things that maybe impede you from having a more contemplative attitude toward nature?

> ### Action
>
> Spend some time outside today, even if just in your own yard or in a city park, and pay close attention to something; ask it to tell you about God, and listen to what it says.

Wednesday, December 3

SAINT FRANCIS XAVIER

Isaiah 25:6–10a; Matthew 15:29–37

"The hand of the Lord will rest on this mountain"

In Scripture, when the hand of the Lord rests on something or on someone, it signifies God is blessing that person or that place. That's how it was before the Fall—the hand of God rested on this whole earth, blessing it. God's hand rested on Adam and on Eve, conveying to them His blessing, His love, His delight in their existence.

Theologians call it "original blessing," the state that mankind was in before the fall, before original sin. It's helpful to think of this: before humanity fell, before our nature was wounded, we were blessed by God. Our existence is good, and not just good, but very good, as God says in Genesis when He creates Adam and Eve.

It can help to picture it: imagine that God the Father is standing in front of you or standing beside you, and His hand, so strong and yet so tenderly loving, rests on your head or on your shoulder, and from His hand on you, you receive strength and peace and clarity about who you are and what you are made for, who you are meant to be. You feel the warmth of His love. You know that, as long as His hand is there, you can face anything.

Because, even though we have fallen, God's hand has never left you. He has not taken back His blessing, not His blessing of the human race, and not His blessing of you, in particular, no matter what your wounds or sins are. He created you, and He holds you in existence. He says that it is very good that you exist, and He blesses you still, blesses you now, blesses you in whatever situation you face today, whatever worries you have, whatever battles you are fighting. His hand rests upon you to strengthen you and affirm you and hold you in existence. So today let yourself be blessed. Let yourself believe that God rests His hand on you, His almighty hand, His loving hand. Let yourself be guided by His hand, gently yet surely, as a father guides his small child, hand resting on his child's head.

Questions for reflection

1. When have you experienced that God rested His hand on you, blessing you? What did that experience teach you about yourself and about God your Father?

2. What things keep you from experiencing that you are blessed by the Father?

3. How have you experienced God's hand guiding you?

Action

Draw or find a picture of a small child with his or her father's hand resting on his or her head, and put it in a place where you will see it throughout the day.

Thursday, December 4

Isaiah 26:1–6; Matthew 7:21, 24–27

"Trust in the Lord forever!"

One of my friends who lives on the streets has a really hard time trusting other people. Perpetually suspicious of others and their motivations, he won't tell anyone else where he is staying on the streets, and when he told me his birth name, he whispered it. He won't say his last name out loud. When a family member committed suicide, he didn't tell anyone about it for over two months. Although he hangs out with others who live outside in the same area, he doesn't open up to them because he is afraid that if he trusts them, he will get hurt. Incapable of trusting, he lives a lonely life, full of suspicion and isolation.

We can't live without trust, at least not well or not for very long. Trust is an essential part of being a human person, because it's a key element of interpersonal relationships, and we were made for relationship.

In the beginning, Adam and Eve could trust in one another, but above all, they could trust in the Lord their God, who walked with them in the cool of the evening, who had made all that they saw, who had made them with loving attention to each detail.

When they trusted in God, they were free, free to enjoy all the good things of the garden, free to love God and one another, free from worry and anxiety, free from fear, free from lies.

Like Adam and Eve, when we trust in God, we can entrust ourselves to him, to his guidance, to his care, and we can listen to and accept all that he tells us, whether we like it or not, because when we trust in him, we know that he loves us and wants what is best for us. When we trust in the Lord, we live in freedom, because we know that all things and every aspect of our lives are in his loving, providential hands.

Questions for reflection

1. In what ways have you entrusted your life, or what aspects of your life, have you entrusted to the Lord? What fruits of trust do you see in these areas?

2. Where do you struggle to trust in the Lord? What fears or anxieties do you bear because of not trusting him more fully?

3. How does not trusting God more fully affect your ability to trust others?

Action

On a small piece of paper, write down some need you have or something you worry about, and in prayer, entrust it to the Lord, placing it behind the crucifix.

Friday, December 5

Isaiah 29:17–24; Matthew 9:27–31

"Jacob shall have nothing to be ashamed of"

When I was in college, one of our education professors told us that it is very common for high school teachers to have recurring nightmares about showing up to class without their pants on. In the dreams, they begin teaching, then notice that all the students are whispering and giggling, and then, all of a sudden, they look down, see that they are naked from the waist down, grab something to cover up, and then run out of the classroom.

Discovering that we are naked in front of others makes us want to run away, to protect ourselves, to hide. We feel vulnerable and embarrassed, exposed and ashamed. But that's not how it was in the beginning. In the beginning, Scripture tells us, Adam and Eve "were naked and without shame."

St. John Paul II calls this "original nakedness," and it doesn't just mean that Adam and Eve were comfortable with naked bodies. It means that there were no barriers to communication between them, that they were safe in each other's presence, because they saw each other as God sees us, not as objects to be used for self–interest, but as other persons, full of dignity and worth and value.

There was nothing to hide from and so nothing was hidden. Rather, they could communicate themselves fully to one another, with simplicity and sincerity. Nothing was covered up, and nothing needed to be uncovered.

Adam and Eve could simply be who they were in the eyes of God, both before God and before one another. There was no duplicity, no double-meanings, no guessing, no insinuating. Their relationship was sincere and honest, open and free.

We are called to relate with that same kind of simplicity and love—not now with naked bodies, but with honest souls, being who we are before God, seeing each other as His beloved sons and daughters, and thus our very own brothers and sisters, worthy of dignity, of respect, of honor, and of love.

Questions for reflection

1. In what relationships and situations do you experience the freedom to be yourself, both before God and before others? Why is this?

2. In what relationships and situations do you hide or cover up aspects of yourself because of shame or fear? Why is this?

3. What tends most to prevent you from recognizing the full dignity of others? Why?

Action

Today honor someone who you usually struggle to see with their full human dignity.

Saturday, December 6

Isaiah 30:19–21, 23–26; Matthew 9:35–10:1, 5a, 6–8

"The Lord will give you the bread you need"

Several years ago, on a mission trip in a poor, mountainous town in the Andes mountains, feeling like the visit in a certain home was going nowhere, we decided to read the famous passage on God's providence from Matthew 6. Though I felt pretty sure by then that nothing was going to come of this, I asked, "Have you ever experienced God's providence?"

The husband and wife looked at each other, then at each of their five children who were sitting with us in the living room of their home. On the table were a loaf of sweet bread that they had shared with us and empty glasses of fruit juice. For a moment, as they exchanged glances, all of us were silent. Then the husband spoke.

"Yes," he said. "We experience this every day." Then he told us that, for the past year, he had been unable to find work, and they had no income. Every night, he and his wife prayed the Our Father together with faith. "And every morning when we get up, we open our gate, and there is a box of food, with just enough for that day. It has been that way for the whole year now. We pray, 'give us this day our daily bread,' and He does."

The three of us who were visiting this home were stunned. We had never heard a testimony of such utter dependence on God and such trust in His providence, and as we left that home, walking back to the school where we were staying, we talked about the faith of this family, doing all they could, but content at the same time to take God at His word.

So often, we tend to worry, to become anxious, to believe that everything depends on us. But the Lord promises that He will give us the bread we need, that He will supply for our every need, that we can trust in Him, because He is a good Father. Jesus tells us that the Father knows what we need before we ask Him.

And this family in the Andes proved to me that it's true, that when we ask for what we need from the Lord, He provides. Not necessarily all that we would like or in the way that we would like, but just what we need, for each day, each moment, each situation.

Questions for reflection

1. When have I experienced that the Lord was providing for my needs on a daily basis? How did this provision happen?

2. What are the things I tend to grasp for or worry about? Why do I find it hard to trust in God's providence in these areas?

3. Have I ever failed to recognize God's providence because it was different from what I wanted?

Action

Today in some concrete way, be the means through which God provides for another's needs.

week two
CAPTURED

In this second week of Advent, we enter into the bad news that we have a powerful Enemy who has captured us, binding us beneath the powers of Sin and Death. These meditations should help to make us more aware of the darkness of sin, of its power in our lives, and of our need for a Savior to rescue us. We can use the meditations this week to help us prepare for a good confession.

Sunday, December 7

ISAIAH 11:1–10
ROMANS 15:4–9
MATTHEW 3:1–12

"They acknowledged their sins"

Years ago, when my niece Danielle was a little girl, on Christmas morning, we walked into her room and found her standing there, with a pair of scissors in one hand and a clump of her own hair in her other hand. She looked at us, eyes big, swallowed hard, and then, all evidence to the contrary, boldly proclaimed, "I didn't tut my hair!"

That's pretty much what happens when God confronts Adam and Eve after the fall. They proclaim their innocence. And not only that, they pass the blame on to others. God says to Adam, "You have eaten, then, from the tree of which I had forbidden you to eat."

What does Adam say? "I'm sorry, God, you're right. I sinned." Nope. He passes the blame on to Eve and to God, saying, "The woman whom you put here with me—she gave me fruit from the tree, so I ate it." He doesn't acknowledge his sin at all—he blames God for it ("it's Your fault, God, You put the woman here with me") and blames Eve for it ("she gave me the fruit—I didn't know what I was doing").

God turns to Eve and says, "Why did you do such a thing?"

Does Eve do any better than Adam? Not at all—she passes the blame on to the serpent. "I'm innocent; he tricked me; it wasn't my fault, I'm not to blame."

Somehow, when the Enemy deceived them, He not only made them doubt God's goodness and goodwill toward them, but also God's merciful nature. Afraid that God will punish them if He "finds out" that they have done wrong, they pass the blame, cover up, try to pretend they are fine, they haven't done anything wrong.

When we believe that God is just waiting to punish us, then it's hard to acknowledge our sins. When we believe that he is just waiting to "smite" us, then it's hard to return to the Father. When we think that we're beyond forgiveness, we pretend we haven't done anything wrong. And yet, all along, our conscience gnaws at us, our heart breaks, our spirit sinks.

All God asks is that we acknowledge our sins and come to Him, for He will abundantly pardon.

And we can face it, because even though the Enemy lords his power over us, his is not the ultimate power. Even though he clothes us again and again in robes of misery, we know that there is One who clothed himself in those robes so He can clothe us later in robes of salvation.

But the way up, as Virgil tells Dante, is the way down. First, we need to recognize and accept our misery, to see it for what it really is, in all of its ugliness and power. And then we will be able to renounce it and ask for redemption from it. So today and this week, let's take a good, hard, clear-sighted look in the mirror, seeing the robe of our misery and all the ways we wear it. It won't lead to despair—we know our Rescuer is on His way.

Questions for reflection

1. What sins do you find most difficult to acknowledge to yourself and before God? Why do these sins seem particularly unforgivable to you? As you look at yourself in the mirror, what don't you like? What do you want to cover up or hide?

2. In what areas of your life are you most tempted to pass the blame on to others? Why is that?

3. When was the last time you acknowledged your sins and your own real responsibility for them? How did the Lord respond to you?

Action

Draw a robe and write on it, with one word for each, the sins and wounds and lies that the Enemy has clothed you in.

Homily Preaching
RESOURCES

Sunday Homily Resources

Again, what is offered below is a suggestion for how a priest or deacon may choose to preach the kerygma this week based on *The Rescue Project*. Last week we looked at the question "Why is there something rather than nothing?" and the word Created. This week we focus on the question "Why is everything so obviously messed up?" and the word Captured.

Summary Points from Rescued
Part 2: Captured
Asking God for the grace of "despair."

The grace of "despair" helps us see how dire our situation is: that we have literally been captured and are in need of rescue.

Key Truths

- ✣ Scripture is a "game film"—it equips us and tells us both "what happened" and "what will always happen."

- ✣ God is all good, but one of the creatures He made chose to rebel against God and us. That creature is the enemy, Satan or the devil, is not an equal rival of God. He is merely a creature.

- ✣ The Enemy is the enemy and that means no human person is. The Devil and demons are real and they desire our death. We are in a spiritual battle!

- ⚜ The enemy's motive for rebellion was envy of the human race. He hates us and has declared war on us. His strategy: to convince us that God is not our loving Father and that we can be happy without God.

- ⚜ Because of Adam and Eve's free choice to believe Satan's lies (the fall), we have been separated from God.

- ⚜ However, we are not just separated from God; humanity is enslaved to Sin and Death.

- ⚜ The Enemy works in certain, consistent ways to keep us enslaved and to destroy our lives: accusation, lies, division, flattery, temptation, confusion, and discouragement.

- ⚜ Humanity is hopeless on its own; understanding this helps us to understand that the Christian life is not simply a matter of morality. You are bound and need grace to be set free. "You will know the truth and the truth will set you free," (John 8:32).

- ⚜ We need to ask Jesus to expose the lies, accusations, and divisions that the enemy has used or is using to wreak havoc in your life. Consider capturing those lies and accusations in writing. Ask God for the grace to hear His loving voice, not the hateful whispers of the enemy.

Consider

Recognizing God's gift of creation compared to the world we live in will quickly raise the question, "Why is everything so obviously messed up?" GK Chesterton said that original sin was the most self–evident of Christian doctrines. We cannot understand and feel deeply the impact of Jesus as Redeemer, Savior, Rescuer without making clear the state of affairs from which He is saving us.

"Now, the serpent was the most cunning of all the animals..." (Genesis 3:1) The reality is that humanity did not fall into Sin on its own power; there was an Enemy who came after us. When Adam and Eve sold our human race into slavery, they did so first because of a loss of trust in God. "Man, tempted by the Devil, let his trust in his creator die in his heart..." (CCC 397).

After the Fall, Sin and Death have come to reign. A great image for the state of humanity in Sin, without grace, is of having been taken, kidnapped, captured from our Father's house. God's great question, "Where are you?" in Genesis 3:9 shows how this dynamic of seeking us who have been taken is present from the beginning. The story of salvation history will be about God coming to get his world back. The protoevangelium in Genesis 3:15 tees up this conquest which the woman's seed will bring; his rescue mission will be about the invasion of the kingdom of death by an immeasurably stronger kingdom.

This dynamic is critical to understand because today we still battle against the Enemy and his attempts to keep us enslaved to Sin and Death. As Pope Francis has reminded us time and again, he still attempts to work in each of our lives in ways that we often do not recognize to keep us from the "life to the full" (John 10:10) which Jesus has come to bring.

Possible Verses for Focus

Isaiah 11:1 – "On that day, a shoot shall sprout from the stump of Jesse, and from his roots a bud shall blossom." Satan brought death and decay; there is no life from a stump. The hope for man was lost in the despair of sin and death. The mentions of the "poor…afflicted…ruthless …wicked" give a clear offering of what the world was living in after the fall.

Romans 15:4 – "For whatever was written previously was written for our instruction, that by endurance and by the encouragement of the scriptures we might have hope." We are called to respond to sin with endurance and encouragement. In "harmony with one another" (v.5) we might hope for a restoration of right relationship with others and God.

Matthew 3:1–12 – "In those days John the Baptist appeared, preaching in the desert of Judea[and] saying, "Repent, for the kingdom of heaven is at hand!" The first quoted word attributed to John is "repent". We were troubled people with wounded hearts and no hope. To repent is to leave what God has prohibited and return to what he commanded. We are offered a change of heart with John's message to "prepare" as a "voice of one crying out in the desert" (v.3), reaching out through desolation to offer a new path.

Monday, December 8

IMMACULATE CONCEPTION

GENESIS 3:9–15, 20;
EPHESIANS 1:3–6, 11–12;
LUKE 1:26–38

"I heard you... but I was afraid"

In our parish, there is a three-year-old boy who is so secure in his parents' love that he hasn't yet learned to be afraid of other people. He is innocent and outgoing, and will walk right up to a stranger and say, "Hi, what's your name?" When you tell him your name, he looks at you and then repeats it to himself. And then he remembers, and calls you by name the next time he sees you. He is innocent and trusting, not yet affected by evil in any way that has caused him to fear.

That's how things were for all of us before the Fall, before Adam and Eve ate of the fruit, before they handed us over to slavery. We didn't know what it was to be afraid, because we were safe in God's love, trusting in His protection and His providence.

But now we live in a different reality. Like our first parents, we too often are afraid of God. We sin or fall and we hide from Him (as if that were even possible!). We shy away from one another, afraid of being found out. We live with an underlying sense of fear: fear of being rejected, fear of being unworthy, fear of proving incompetent, fear of failing, fear of commitment. So many fears!

We hear God speak, and rather than returning to Him, we may hide from Him or try to run from Him. Our fear has distorted

His voice. Rather, our fear has distorted our ability to hear His voice. Instead of hearing a loving Father trying to bring back His children, we hear a threatening voice. Instead of thinking that God is watching us and finding that reassuring, we hear it as dooming, because we assume God is watching us in order to punish us.

How far removed from the truth! If only today we would hear His voice, His voice of love, His voice of sorrow for our sins, His voice of power to transform us, then we wouldn't let fear harden our hearts. If only we would hear His voice as it really is, we would reveal to him our nakedness and our woundedness, our sins and our failings, like a little child running to his mother or father to show how he scraped his knee.

If today we would hear His voice as it really is, we would stop hiding, we would stop cowering, and we would turn back to Him with all our hearts. And we would find out the truth again, that He is a loving Father, and let him take us up in His arms and bind up all our wounds and forgive all our iniquities.

Questions for reflection

1. In what ways does fear show up in your life? What are the ways you tend to act out of fear rather than out of love?

2. What things in your life do you try to hide from God or from others? What are you afraid would happen if you were to reveal them?

3. How do you hear God asking Adam, "Where are you?" What tone of voice? What does that reveal to you about your image of God?

> ### Action
> Make an act of renunciation. Take one of the specific fears you have, write it on a piece of paper, attach that paper to a rock, and throw it into a body of water.

Tuesday, December 9

Isaiah 40:1–11; Matthew 18:12–14

*"Will he not leave the ninety–nine
and go in search of the stray?"*

A few years back, the story of a Merino sheep in Australia made international headlines, when he was found after many years of having wandered from the flock. Baarack, the sheep, was barely eking out an existence, his face and legs nearly completely hidden under 78 pounds of wool. Rescued, Baarack was shorn, and could again begin to live a normal life, gaining back a healthy body weight, living again among the flock, attended to by the shepherd.

We laugh at stories like Baarack the sheep's. But his story isn't so different from our own. We, too, have wandered from the fold, some of us for many years. And in our wanderings, our wool continues to grow, that is, we accumulate sins and wounds and burdens, and soon we are carrying about a weight that is far too great for us, and we can do nothing about it.

Sometimes we try. We think of some way to get ourselves out of the mess of some wrongdoing, but that almost always involves deception or lies or cover up, which just adds to the mess. So rather than returning to the flock and the shepherd, we wander farther away, convinced that we can only come back when we can make things right, when we can fix whatever we've broken, when we can prove that we deserve to be in the sheepfold.

And left to our own devices, we will wander forever, burdened under the ever growing weight of our sin, interiorly starving, eking out a meager existence until we can just make things right.

But Baarack couldn't shear himself, and neither can we. We need the Shepherd to come and find us, to take us back to the fold, to get out the shears of His mercy, and to start clipping away, until all the extra wool has come off of us. And that's what can happen with a good confession. We can stand still, let the Lord find us, and then, no longer trying to fix things or cover things up or remove things on our own, just let Him see us exactly as we are, buried under the burden of our sins. As we confess our sins, He will be faithful and just, and will shear them all away from us and return us to the fold.

So today, let's decide to stop running and hiding and trying on our own to make right what we've done wrong. Let's tell the Good Shepherd that we need him to pick us up and carry us back to the fold and remove the burdens we bear.

Questions for reflection

1. When have you tried to fix your mistakes or sins on your own? What was the result?

2. What is the longest you've gone without confession? How heavy did that burden become?

3. In what ways do you tend to rely on rather than turn to the Lord for mercy?

Action
Take a wisp of wool or cotton (something that can look like wool) and carry it with you today. Each time you look at it or feel it, think of the sins that you carry because you are trying to fix things yourself.

Wednesday, December 10

ISAIAH 40:25–31; MATTHEW 11:28–30

"My yoke is easy"

A while ago a priest I know shocked a bunch of college students when he told them that living according to the Gospel is, in the long run, the easiest thing to do, easier than living in submission to our own passions and the changing criteria of the world. The students didn't quite know what to make of it. All their lives they'd heard that following Jesus is hard, that it is only constant cross, that it means giving up all they enjoy and living a life of toil and drudgery.

And that's one of the biggest lies that Satan tells us in order to keep us from finding rest for our souls. Satan tells us that following Jesus is too hard, that Jesus' teachings are burdensome and restrictive, that we won't be able to carry the yoke. It's simply too hard, he says. Look how easy it is to just do what you want to do when you want it. Look how much freedom you have if you just do things your own way.

And we buy it, so much of the time. We think about fighting against a specific temptation, and then we agree with the lie: "that's too hard, and beside it's not such a big deal." Or we decide to incorporate more prayer time in our lives, but then the Enemy tells us we don't have the strength to give up our screen time for it. Or we choose to reconcile with someone, and the Enemy tells us that we are going to get used, hurt, rejected again.

But then we are left with the aftermath of our refusal to follow Christ, and we find ourselves shut out of the garden still, with no other way back home. We've been wandering our whole lives, trying to do things our own way, letting our passions or ambitions guide our paths, and where has it gotten us? Are we happy? Fulfilled? Free? Are our souls at rest?

That's what Jesus promises: rest for our souls. On our own, we are restless, anxious. Even the best of us, the most seemingly balanced of us, without Jesus, live with restless anxiety of heart—or we live trying to silence the restlessness of our hearts with shopping or food or alcohol or drugs or travel or diversions of varying sorts.

Satan is the liar, not Jesus. Truth himself speaks truly, St. Thomas Aquinas wrote, or there's nothing true. And Satan was a liar from the beginning. So who do you choose today to believe?

Questions for reflection

1. In what ways do you believe the lie that following Jesus is too hard? What spiritual steps have you not taken because you are buying into that lie?

2. In what ways have you found rest for your soul in following Jesus? How does that experience differ from previous experiences?

3. What are the things you do to try to keep from paying attention to your own inner restlessness?

Action

Make a decision today to listen to Jesus' promise in just one area of your life, and fight against the lie in that area.

Thursday, December 11

Isaiah 41:13-20; Matthew 11:11-15

"To what shall I compare this generation?"

A dear friend of mine recently confessed to me that neither the meth he injects nor the weed he smokes help him with his pain, yet he keeps using them though he doesn't actually experience a physical dependency on them. He said, "It helps me built Tetris walls in my mind, so I don't have to think about things." The drug-built Tetris walls, which he has to rebuild day after day, hide years of abuse, abandonment, betrayal—sufferings so awful that only hell could have devised them. What my friend is really seeking are peace and healing as he injects poisons into his body so he doesn't have to face the memories that torment him and still squeeze his soul.

Most of us have our own version of his vain searches, things we go back to again and again seeking meaning or pleasure or love or to feel better about ourselves or to not feel pain. Maybe we don't shoot meth or smoke weed, but if we're honest with ourselves, we, too, have our own addictions, our repeated sins, the ways we seek water in vain. Our souls are parched with thirst, terrible thirst, desperate thirst. And though deep down we know that the sin we're addicted to doesn't really help, we "drink" it anyway, not trusting that we will make it to life-giving water if we wait, afraid we will die in the desert of our past pain or current anguish.

The Lord today invites us to hear His promise: "I, the God of Israel, will not forsake them. I will open rivers on the bare heights and fountains in the broad valleys. I will turn the desert into a marshland, and dry ground into springs of water."

Yes, the desert is a place of desperate thirst, but it is not forever. Yes, the wounds in our souls can feel unbearable, but they are not beyond healing. Yes, the memories can make us feel all alone or totally unworthy of love, but they are not the final word. The Lord Himself will come, and out of His heart will flow rivers of living water to heal our hurting hearts. Let us ask for the grace to trust and to wait.

Questions for reflection

1. What are your vain searches? And what, exactly, are you seeking when you turn to these things?

2. When do you find it most difficult not to give in to the temptation to whatever addictive behavior you struggle with? Try to name what is at the root of it (fear, not trusting God, self-loathing, etc.)

3. When have you experienced the Lord giving you real water for your soul's thirst? How did that living water heal you or transform you? Where do you most long to see wisdom vindicated by?

Action

Every time you take a drink of water today, imagine that the Lord is giving your soul to drink of whatever healing or peace or joy or love you need in order not to turn to your vain searches.

Friday, December 12

OUR LADY OF GUADALUPE

ZECHARIAH 2:14-17; OR REVELATION
11:19A, 12:1-6A, 10AB; LUKE 1:26–38

"The dragon stood before the woman… to devour her child"

Commentators read this passage in Revelation, and rightly identify the woman as both the Virgin Mary and the Church. But in some ways, the woman in this passage is also the woman who gave birth to each one of us, because from the moment of our birth, the Enemy has been trying to devour us, to destroy us. We often forget about him, but he has been there since our first breath, plotting and planning and seeking when and how he might destroy us.

It's not so hard to recognize if you look at what happens in the world today. Research shows that somewhere around 1 out of 4 girls and 1 out of 6 boys are sexually abused before the age of 18. In the U.S. alone, 3.6 million to 10 million children are exposed to adult domestic violence each year. More than 20% of 8th graders in the US have tried illicit drugs at least once. This is not accidental. And it's very personal.

Each of these numbers represents a person loved by God but whom the Enemy is seeking to devour. And he has been at this in our own lives, too, from the beginning. Those who wronged you in life, whether it was to the level of abuse or not, were not working alone. The lies that were sown in your soul—that you are unworthy, unlovable, all alone, powerless, weak, incapable, worthless, dirty—those were spoken to you, and continue to be spoken to you, by the Enemy.

When we fail to recognize him, he works in one of his favorite ways, hiding in the shadows, making us believe the negative thoughts and self-rejecting feelings are just part of our own psychology. When we fail to recognize him, he devises and strategizes more and more ways of binding us, of entrapping us, of enslaving us—sometimes to our more bodily passions and desires, sometimes to our desires for prestige or recognition or power.

So it's utterly important that we remember that he is one of the actors on stage, or we will fail to understand who God is and what He has done, and fail to understand our own bondage and the bondage of those held in captivity by the Enemy.

Not a single one of us can pull ourselves up by our bootstraps—that's one of the lies he tells us, in fact, that we should be able to get ourselves out of the mess we find ourselves in. Not a single one of us has the power to overthrow this Enemy.

But our Redeemer is coming. Our rescue is at hand. So let's take a good, hard look at our lives and see how the Enemy has been trying to destroy us, so we can value that rescue for all that it's worth.

Questions for reflection

1. Looking back at your life, what are the earliest events where you can detect the Enemy trying to destroy?

2. In what ways has the Enemy tried to destroy and devour you? What are the tactics he has been using on you your whole life?

3. Where do you most need Jesus to come in and rescue you and bind up the Enemy?

Action

Tie a string or cord on your wrist today, with a knot for each of the ways you identify Satan working in your life, and ask Jesus to come and set you free.

Saturday, December 13

SAINT LUCY

SIRACH 48:1–4, 9–11; MATTHEW. 17:9A, 10–13

"To turn back the hearts of the fathers to their sons"

One of the names for the Enemy is the devil, diablos, the divider. The Enemy knows that, if he can divide us, if he can separate us from one another, it is easier to pick us off, to capture us, to devour us. And there is no where that he more likes to work this division than in our families. If he can destroy families, he has a better chance of destroying children, and the younger he begins to work in our lives, the more devastating his work can be.

And since we have mostly forgotten about him or ignored him in this country, he has been able to work in our families with devastating results. Every hour in the US, there are 86 divorces, with the current national divorce rate at about 42%. Nearly 1 in 2 children will witness their parents' divorce. Nearly 21% of children in the U.S. are being raised without a father.

Studies show that children who grow up without their father are more likely to be angry, depressed, and insecure, more likely to struggle in school, more likely to get incarcerated, more likely to use drugs, and more likely to commit suicide. Sociologists are quick to link the increasing deaths of despair, especially among young men, to growing up without a father.

Without a father, it's hard to understand God as Father, and that's part of the Enemy's plan. If he can make us believe that the Father might walk out on us at any minute, or already has walked out on us, he can convince us that we really are all alone in the world, without meaning, without purpose, without guidance, without security. If he can convince us that the Father isn't really there for us, then he can convince us that we have only ourselves to depend on, while at the same time convincing us that we can't do what we need to in order to grow or even just to get by.

Attacking fathers, he has managed to separate families. Separating families, he has managed to pick off the most vulnerable.

Oh how great is our need for one who can reveal the Father to us!

Questions for reflection

1. In what ways has the Enemy lied to you about God as your Father? Why have you believed those lies?

2. What did your earthly father show you about who and how God is? What did he fail to show you?

3. How is the Enemy seeking to divide your family right now? What can you do to withstand his tactics?

Action

Reach out today to a father in your life, whether your own father, your child's father, your priest, or someone who has been a father to you, and tell them how they have shown God the Father to you.

week three
RESCUED

As we so clearly saw last week, we desperately need someone greater than our Enemy to rescue us from him and from the powers of sin and death. Jesus, by his incarnation, passion, death and resurrection, has done just that. This week's meditations will take us to the heart of the meaning of this season: God the Son has come to overthrow the strong man and set us free.

Sunday, December 14

ISAIAH 35:1–6A, 10

JAMES 5:7–10

MATTHEW 11:2–11

"Here is your God . . . he comes to save you"

If you're like me, you're a little tired on this Third Sunday of Advent, tired of looking at all the ways the Enemy holds you captive, tired of recognizing how often he lies to you and you fall for it, tired of seeing the sin in your life, tired of experiencing your own weakness to change. And maybe even a little tempted to discouragement. Yuck, all of this, and it's still there! Why can't I ever change? When will I ever break free?

But maybe those are the wrong questions. Maybe I haven't changed because I am relying on myself. Maybe I can't break free because I think I have to do what only God can do for me. Maybe I forget I need a Savior, that the best I can do in these floodwaters is to tread water and wait for rescue.

And today's readings are like balm for our souls, a powerful reminder that we can't and don't have to save ourselves. "The coming of the Lord is at hand," James says. The Lord is at hand, the Lord, the Almighty, the Unconquerable, the Victor, He is here, He is coming, and He is on our side.

He comes to save us, Isaiah says. He comes with vindication: He comes to defend us against denial or our dignity, against the accusations and attacks of the Enemy. He comes with divine recompense, comes to make up for all we have suffered, comes to compensate us with his mercy for all that we've lost in our bondage to the Enemy.

He comes as our defender, as our shield, as our protector. He comes as our Savior, to rescue us from the hand of our oppressor. And He comes to recompense us in ways we cannot even begin to imagine, to pour his infinite, tender, powerful love into all the wounds of our souls. He is coming. He comes to save us.

Questions for reflection

1. Think of all the ways the Enemy attacks with lies or temptations, and imagine Jesus vindicating you, protecting you and shielding you from the attacks. What changes in your inner response when you know the Lord is protecting you?

2. You are probably well aware of the wounds in your soul, all that has been taken from you through the harm you have suffered in life. What does it mean that the Lord is going to recompense you for all of that?

3. In what ways do you most need to experience the salvation of our God this Christmas?

Action

Read Isaiah 35:4 again, out loud, but adding your name, like this: "Say to _____whose heart is frightened: Be strong, fear not! Here is your God, _____, he comes with vindication; with divine recompense, he comes to save you,_____."
Write your name in the blanks, and read it again, then again, then again. Repeat it until you believe it.

Sunday Homily Resources

What is offered below is a suggestion for how a priest or deacon may choose to preach the kerygma this week based on *The Rescue Project*. Last week we looked at the question "Why is everything so obviously messed up?" and the word Captured. This week we focus on the question "What, if anything, has God done about it?" and the word Rescued.

Summary Points from Rescued
Part 3: Rescued

Asking God for the grace of unshakeable confidence in Jesus as Lord of heaven and earth.

Key Truths

- ⚜ We need clarity and alignment on why Jesus came: God's response to our captivity to sin is shocking and unexpected.

- ⚜ Why did Jesus come? He "landed" on the earth to fight our enemy, the devil. In short, He came to rescue us and release us from our chains.

- ⚜ What he was doing on the Cross: showing us God's love, taking on punishment and remitting sin, defeating the Enemy and attacking Sin and Death.

- ⚜ Jesus is not just hunted, He's the hunter; He's not just the victim, but the aggressor. He is the ultimate Ambush Predator. The crucifixion could not have happened unless God wanted it to.

- ⚜ What difference the Resurrection makes: Jesus has humiliated the enemy, destroyed death, transferred us to His kingdom, given us access to the Father, recreated us, rendered sin impotent, and given us authority over the enemy.

- ⚜ The following week we will ask how we should respond, and what God is now sending us to do.

- ⚜ Consider: connection to Our Lady of Guadalupe – woman clothed with the sun – how she rescued the native people of America and continues to be an instrument of rescuing people today for her Son, Jesus Christ.

Consider

This message picks up in hope from the previous thoughts on Captured. This condition of Sin and Death into which we have been captured...has God just left us there? Has he done anything about it? The creativity of this homily is found in getting life–long Catholics to view the Passion and Death of Jesus Christ in a new way, to consider from a different angle what the Cross really means, to help them move beyond platitudes. On the Cross, Jesus is taking on punishment for sin and, in choosing to remain there, showing us the love of the Father in the depths to which love has driven him in dying for us "while we were still sinners." (Romans 5:8).

Yet, He is not just victim on the Cross but Conqueror. "No one takes (my life) from me but I lay it down on my own." (John 10:18). Jesus, in the Incarnation, is able to conquer Sin and Death by taking them into Himself and destroying them forever. This is the trap He lays for the Devil and how He binds the "strongman" (Mark 3:27). This is how our King has come to do battle for us, and rescue us from the captivity in which He has found us.

Possible Verses for Focus

Isaiah 35:1–3 – "The desert and parched land will exult" … the beginning of this passage repeats the promise of new life and restoration to original glory and splendor in creation. "Be strong, fear not! Here is your God, he comes with vindication, with divine recompense he comes to save you" (v.4); we're offered a very clear message of God's promise to rescue all those "ransomed" will be given "everlasting joy" and "gladness" (v.10)

James 5:7 – "Be patient, brothers and sisters, until the coming of the Lord." There is no doubt or speculation, only a request for patience in the assurance of Christ's rescue mission. "Make your hearts firm because the coming of the Lord is at hand." (v.8)

Matthew 11:4–6 – "Jesus said to them in reply, "Go and tell John what you hear and see: the blind regain their sight, the lame walk, lepers are cleansed, the deaf hear, the dead are raised, and the poor have the good news proclaimed to them. And blessed is the one who takes no offense at me." We will know Jesus by the fruits of his love and mercy. He asks us to pay attention to those that encounter him; to recognize him in the miraculous works of God. No one that truly encounters Christ is unchanged. He is the Word, but asks to be known by his word alone. He humbly points back to God, his merciful Father that desires healing and restoration for each of us.

Matthew 11:10 – "Behold, I am sending my messenger ahead of you; he will prepare your way before you." Not only does God plan to rescue us, but his plan for redemption includes continued promises and opportunities for preparation. His love is rooted in the assurance of ultimately overcoming all that brings us pain and death in this life by taking on Satan in the battle for our souls.

St. Leo the Great, Sermon 22 – "When, therefore, the merciful and almighty Saviour so arranged the commencement of His human course as to hide the power of His Godhead which was inseparable from His manhood under the veil of our weakness, the crafty foe was taken off his guard and he thought that the nativity of the Child, Who was born for the salvation of mankind, was as much subject to himself as all others are at their birth. For he saw Him crying and weeping, he saw Him wrapped in swaddling clothes, subjected to circumcision, offering the sacrifice which the law required. And then he perceived in Him the usual growth of boyhood ... Meanwhile, he inflicted insults, multiplied injuries, made use of curses, affronts, blasphemies, abuse, in a word, poured upon Him all the force of his fury and exhausted all the varieties of trial: and knowing how he had poisoned man's nature, had no conception that He had no share in the first transgression Whose mortality he had ascertained by so many proofs. The unscrupulous thief and greedy robber persisted in assaulting Him Who had nothing of His own, and in carrying out the general sentence on original sin, went beyond the bond on which he rested, and required the punishment of iniquity from Him in Whom he found no fault. And thus the malevolent terms of the deadly compact are annulled, and through the injustice of an overcharge the whole debt is canceled. The strong one is bound by his own chains, and every device of the evil one recoils on his own head. When the prince of the world is bound, all that he held in captivity is released. Our nature cleansed from its old contagion regains its honorable estate, death is destroyed by death, nativity is restored by nativity: since at one and the same time redemption does away with slavery, regeneration changes our origin, and faith justifies the sinner."

Monday, December 15

NUMBERS 24:2–7; 15–17A; MATTHEW 21:23–27

"Then I shall tell you by what authority I do these things."

There's a scene in the Gospels where a centurion comes up to Jesus and asks him to heal his servant at home, saying that he doesn't need Jesus to come to his house, because Jesus can just say the word, and his servant will be healed. The centurion explains his faith through the lens of authority; he understands authority, because he gives a command to a soldier under him and the soldier does it. And the centurion himself has to obey orders from those who have authority over him. What he is professing is that Jesus has authority over life and death, that all things are subject to Jesus.

The Greek word for authority has several meanings, but what the centurion recognizes in Jesus, and what the Jewish leaders don't want to recognize, is that Jesus has the freedom and the right to decide and to act without any obstacles, and that Jesus has the capability and power to take action, to make His actions bear fruit.

But they come and ask Him about authority in a different sense, the authority given to Him from somewhere else, a kind of delegated authority. The centurion recognizes that he has a delegated authority, but that Jesus' authority isn't delegated, but somehow total, somehow complete. There is no one over him telling him what he can and cannot do, but Jesus himself decides and has the power to do whatever he decides.

We need to be more like the centurion. It seems to me that sometimes we go to Jesus in prayer without much faith in His authority. We can think that circumstances condition how he can respond. We can believe that the obstacles of the Enemy are too great. We can even think that our own weakness could somehow block the power of the Lord.

But the authority of Jesus has no limits. He can command the storm to stop, the lame to walk, the deaf to hear, the dumb to speak, the blind to see. He can tell the bread to be multiplied and feed five thousand from just five loaves. He can tell the dead to rise. He can tell the demons to flee. Nothing and no one can limit his power, the power of his word.

So today let's get out of the way and see what He can do. Let's come before Him in the faith of the centurion, knowing that all He has to do is say the word, and whatever He wants to happen will happen. And let's present Him our needs and the needs of others with faith in His unlimited authority to act in our lives and in this world.

Questions for reflection

1. Where do you tend to think of the Lord's power or authority as limited? Why?

2. What keeps you from praying with the faith of the centurion?

Action

Spend 10 minutes in vocal prayer telling the Lord that you believe in His authority, in His power, and then, praising Him for what he can do, intercede for Him to act with all His authority in the life of someone close to you.

Tuesday, December 16

ZEPHANIAH 3:1-2, 9-13; MATTHEW 21:28-32

"He changed his mind and went"

How could tax collectors and prostitutes—or in other words, the worst of sinners—enter the Kingdom of God before the religious elite, those who meticulously sought to keep the law? Or not even before others, but at all?

One of the effects on us of others' judgments of us is that we tend to internalize them, to believe that their judgments are somehow definitive. And we've done the same with the Enemy's pronouncements about who we are. He always tries to define us and bind us to the worst things we've done, to turn our sins into our identity, until we come to see ourselves as the wrong things we've done. We think we are sinners and only sinners.

But what Jesus shows in this parable is that it's never too late to change, never too late to undergo conversion, never too late to experience metanoia, or, in other words, to change our minds, to change what we believe about who we are. When we believe the lies of the Enemy and the judgments of others, we believe that we cannot do God's will.

But when we believe what Jesus says about who we are, that we are beloved sons and daughters of the Father, and that none of our previous refusals to do the Father's will, and not even all of those refusals taken together, can change that deepest identity, beloved, then we can change our minds and repent and go do the Father's will.

It doesn't matter if you have been hardened in your false belief about yourself for decades, or if you have never before thought of yourself as beloved. All that matters is that today you hear the voice of the Lord, telling you who you are, a beloved child of God, and that you live as such. It's never too late to believe in the Lord's love. It's never too late to let go of the lies. It's never too late to change our "no" to God's will into a "yes."

It's never too late, because our Rescuer has come, has burst asunder the shackles of our shame, has lifted us out of the depths of our sin, and has told us again who we are and Whose we are: beloved sons and daughters of the Father, made by love, for love

Questions for reflection

1. Is there any area in your life where you think you cannot change? What is beneath that belief?

2. If you believed that Jesus gives you the power to go and do the Father's will, would anything in your life look different? How so?

3. What can you do today to live as a beloved child of the Father?

Action

Make a list of 10 ways you have said "no" to God's will in the past, and choose one of those areas to say "Yes" to Him today.

Wednesday, December 17

Genesis 49:2, 8–10; Matthew 1:1–17

"The book of the genealogy of Jesus Christ"

One of the most amazing things about the first chapter of Matthew is the way it highlights shameful situations in the family of Jesus. There is no writing over of the family tree, no trying to erase or cover up the shameful things of the past, no glazing over the sins of his human ancestors. No, it's all there, the glorious and upright, and the wicked and shameful. It's amazing, because you might think that, just as God became incarnate of a sinless Virgin, he might have kept his whole family safe, allowing himself to be born into a family without any of the usual burdens and sins and negative situations of a family tree.

But that's not what he did. God Himself became incarnate in a human family, with a history of woundedness, a story full of sin and its consequences. And the genealogy even highlights them: Tamar, who disguised herself as a prostitute so Judah would provide children for her. Rahab, the harlot who shelters the Israelite spies. Ruth, the foreigner. Solomon, son of the woman with whom David committed adultery and whose husband he had killed. Not exactly bright spots on the family tree. Not exactly the kind of thing you want to have known about your ancestors.

So why is it proclaimed here? What makes it good news?

The good news is that God became incarnate in a human family with a history as wounded and messed up as your own family's or my own family's. And He didn't try to cover up or deny the past; instead He took up the past, embraced it, bore it to the cross, and redeemed it. All those wounds and sins and shame in

His family tree, He redeemed. And all the wounds and sins and shame in our own family trees He also redeems.

His salvation reaches back all the way to Adam and Eve. His salvation reaches back and redeems the sin of Judah and Tamar, of Rahab, of David and Bathsheba. And His salvation reaching into your own life somehow reaches back and redeems whatever it is in your family history that needs redemption. So let's entrust to Him today our families, whatever that history may look like, knowing that He can redeem everything.

Questions for reflection

1. What family sin in your heritage most needs redemption?

2. In your own family history, your own upbringing, what most needs to be touched by the grace of the Incarnation? Do you believe Jesus can redeem it?

3. What would it mean for you to believe that Jesus can and has redeemed your family history? How would you view your family and yourself differently?

Action

Make a family tree, whatever the family history you know, and then place it today in the empty manger, making an act of faith that through the incarnation, Jesus has redeemed it.

Thursday, December 18

Jeremiah 23:5-8; Matthew 1:18-25

"He will save his people from their sins"

One of my dearest friends on the streets has been shaped by sin his whole life. As a young child, he suffered pretty badly in his own family, from the sins of his father who abandoned him, from the sins of his mother who was with many different men, from the sins of his uncle who beat him, from the sins of his older siblings who abused him. It set him up for his own life of sin, leading to alcohol and drug use in his teens, his own sexual sin, and eventually leading him to the streets, where his life has included opioid abuse, fights, theft, a great devaluing of his own life and the life of others.

When I pray for his salvation, I'm not just praying for the Lord to snatch him from the Enemy at the end of his life and get him to heaven. I'm not just praying for him not to get punished, but for him to experience salvation here and now, salvation from sin, from all the sins committed against him and all the sins he has committed. I'm praying for him to experience new life, fullness of life: freedom from addiction, healing from abuse, repentance and conversion of heart, and all that it would mean to be healed from the incredible damage that sin has done in his life and experience union with God.

Jesus didn't become man, suffer and die on the cross, just to give us a bit of fire insurance. No, He became man and suffered all that He suffered in order to free us from the power of Satan, in order to save us from our sins, in order to heal all the wounds caused by sin, in order to restore in us the image of God which we are.

It's not cheap. It's not a quick fix. It's a process of transformation, until we look like Jesus, until the Father sees in us the image of His Son. And Jesus came to do that, and the promise is that He will do it, "he will save his people from their sins."

Today let's open ourselves to that salvation, wherever we need it in our lives. And let's pray for that salvation in those who we see have been wounded by sin. And let's pray with confidence, claiming the promise the angel made to Joseph, "He will save his people from their sins."

Questions for reflection

1. How do you usually think of salvation? Based on the idea of salvation, how do you relate to Jesus as your Savior?

2. Where in your own life do you most need to experience the fullness of salvation right now?

3. Where do you see the damage caused by sin most evidently in your family or community? How can you pray for the Lord to save his people?

Action

Spend 10 minutes today in intercession for the salvation of someone whose life you see has been damaged by sin.

Friday, December 19

JUDGES 13:2–7, 24–25A; LUKE 1:5–25

"You will have joy and gladness"

The Catholic writer Leon Bloy once wrote in a letter to a friend, "Joy is the infallible sign of God's presence." It's a sign that is all throughout prophetic literature announcing the coming of the Messiah, even the desert will exult and rejoice, breaking into bloom when the Lord comes. Over and over, the Lord says through his prophets, "Rejoice!" At the birth of Jesus, joy is the predominant feeling: the joy of the angels, the joy of the shepherds, the joy of Mary and Joseph, the joy of the magi.

In fact, when the angels announce to the shepherds that Jesus has been born, they say, "We bring you glad tidings of great joy which shall be for all people: today, a Savior has been born." Today, your Rescuer has arrived. Today, the One who will set you free and give you a new life has landed in your world. Today everything changes.

The joy that comes from being rescued, from being in relationship with Jesus, from living a new life, is not the same as any other joy or happiness in our lives. It's a joy that's not dependent on circumstances, that doesn't fluctuate with our moods, that remains even in times of suffering or trial. It's the joy of living in the presence of God, of being with God, of God being with us.

It's a participation, already, in what predominates in heaven, where the Father rejoices constantly, rejoices over each one of us in love, rejoices each time someone experiences rescue, rejoices, each time a wayward son or daughter comes home.

It can be helpful to gauge our joy, because our joy just might be the measure of our awareness of the Lord's presence in our lives. Wherever we experience that we are in his presence, we will have joy. Wherever we absent ourselves from his presence, we will lack joy. So let's ask for the grace today to live with a spirit of rejoicing, to recognize that we have been rescued, and to live in the presence of our God.

Questions for reflection

1. How much is your life marked by joy? Have others commented on your joy?

2. How expressive are you of the joy that comes from knowing God is with you? What steps can you take to let that joy radiate more fully?

3. Do you tend to think of God as joyful and rejoicing? Why or why not?

Action

Write the word "REJOICE!" in big, bold letters, and put it somewhere you will see it, especially where you most need to remember to be joyful.

Saturday, December 20

Isaiah 7:10–14; Luke 1:26–38

"Do not be afraid"

When the angel Gabriel appears to Mary, right after greeting her, he first tells her, "Do not be afraid." Why not? An archangel has just appeared in her room, a being intensely more powerful and of such beauty and brightness that she has never imagined anything like it. And he has just addressed her in a way that she has never been addressed before, with a voice a clear as a bell and as sharp as a blade. And she is just a poor teenage girl in a tiny town in Israel. Who is she, that some being of this sort should appear to her and speak to her as he speaks to her?

"Do not be afraid." Not that the angel doesn't say, "Don't feel afraid," but rather, "don't be afraid." And that's what the Lord says to us each day, because 365 times in Scripture, some version of this command is given: "Do not be afraid." Again, not, "don't feel afraid," but "don't be afraid."

Why the importance of this distinction between being afraid and feeling afraid?

Well, God knows us. He knows we are small creatures, vulnerable creatures, that since the Fall we have been beset by fear, exposed as we are now to all kind of dangers because of the disorder that we brought into creation. And He knows that fear is a powerful feeling, one that can easily dominate our hearts, so He tells us not to let it.

Don't be afraid, He says to us. Don't be afraid. I know you feel afraid, but don't let that feeling take over. Don't stand in your fear and live out of your fear. Don't let fear determine how you see the world, how you see others, how you see yourself. Don't be afraid; when you feel afraid, stand in faith.

Because, ultimately, the answer of why we don't need to be afraid is in the greeting of the angel to Mary, which, because of her consent, is now true for all of us: "The Lord is with you."

The Lord is with you, so don't be afraid. The Lord, Almighty God, ruler of heaven and earth, captain of all the hosts of heaven, the one who has defeated sin and death and Satan, the Lord Jesus is with you. No one and nothing can withstand His power. No one and nothing can defeat Him. And He is with you. So don't be afraid.

Questions for reflection

1. When and in what situations do you tend to let fear dominate your heart? Why?

2. Imagine Jesus going with you, with all the hosts of angels behind him, to face the thing or situation that most causes you to fear. What happens to your fear?

3. How has living a new life after experiencing rescue changed your level of fear and way of facing fearful situations?

Action
Write down all the things that cause you to fear, and over all of them, in bold letters write, "The Lord is with you; do not be afraid."

week four
RESPONSE

Rescued by Jesus, who has come into this world to restore all things, we are invited to respond to his coming and to all that he has done. In these last few days of Advent and the first week of Christmas, we will meditate on how we are called to respond to so great a love, to so powerful a salvation, to mighty a Savior. As we pray this week, let's ask for the grace to respond wholeheartedly, to let this season and these meditations bear fruit, not only in our own lives, but in the lives of those to whom the Lord sends us.

Sunday, December 21

Isaiah 7:10–14
Romans 1:1–7
Matthew 1:18–24

"Ask for a sign from God"

What would you do if you were in Ahaz's shoes, if you knew God said to you, "Ask me for a sign. Ask me to do something for you that seems impossible—something deep as the netherworld or high as the sky. Just ask." What would you do?

Or maybe a better question would be what do you do? God has come, He has said to you, "Whatever you ask for in my name, I will do." He has come, and He has said, "Ask, and you shall receive."

What does your prayer look like? Do you ask God for things? Do you ask him for big things? Do you ask him for seemingly impossible things?

Why not?

I think we often don't ask for big things from God in prayer, not from a false piety, like Ahaz, but from a lack of faith in his power to do immeasurably more than all we can ask or imagine. Or from fear of being disappointed if He doesn't answer our prayer. Or from a sense of our own unworthiness to stand before God and ask Him to show up in big ways in our lives or the lives of those we love.

Sometimes I think we have a small god, that we have let the discoveries of the immensity of this creation diminish our idea of who God is, when really he holds all of this creation, all 93+ billion light years of it, in His hands. And He spoke it all into existence out of nothing. Why would He be unable to do whatever thing we need, when we are such a tiny little speck of this vast creation? How could any problem that one of us faces be too big for the God who holds the whole universe in the palm of His hand, who daily speaks new stars into being?

God can say, "let it be deep as the netherworld or high as the sky" because all of creation is His, so nothing can be too big for Him, no request too bold for him, no thing impossible for Him. And he showed us this himself, when he became one of us, walked and breathed and ate and laughed and wept and worked and lived among us. He healed lepers with a word, cured blindness with a touch of the hand, stopped a years'-long hemorrhage with the tassel of his garment, raised the dead, overthrew the powers of Sin and Death. What could possibly be too big or too difficult for Him in any one of our lives?

I dare you: ask. Don't hold back. Ask. Don't give up. Ask boldly. Ask big. Ask bravely. Ask. God Himself invites you: ask.

And His will for us is not only in big decisions, not only in who we marry (or if we marry), in what job we take, in whether we buy that house or not. It's in our daily life. So what is His will for us?

Obedience: to listen daily to His word and then to act on it, to let Him take the reins of our life, to let Him tell us who we are and what we are made for, to let Him lead us where and when and how He wants us to go. Each day, in Scripture, God is speaking to us. Each day, in Scripture, He is revealing His will for us. Each day, through listening to Him in Scripture, we have the chance to respond just as He wants us to respond that day, in a way that is pleasing to Him.

So as we go through these meditations in this last week, let's say simply when we come to pray, "Here I am, Lord, I come to do Your will." And then let's do, promptly, whatever it is that he tells us.

Questions for reflection

1. When you are in need of something from God that seems impossible to you, do you ask him for it? Why or why not? And if you ask, how do you ask?

2. When have you seen God respond to prayer in powerful ways? Why do you think he responded to those prayers in that way?

3. When God hasn't answered your prayer with a yes, have you ever responded by asking more boldly and more incessantly? Why or why not?

Action

Wherever you pray in your home, or on a piece of paper in your Bible, write down today's date, and then write down a petition for something that seems impossible. Ask God for it each day until you see His answer. Then write down the date He answers it and how He answers it.

Homily Preaching
RESOURCES

Sunday Homily Resources

What is offered below is a suggestion for how a priest or deacon may choose to preach the kerygma this week based on *The Rescue Project*. Last week we looked at the question "What, if anything, has God done about it?" and the word Rescued. This week we focus on the question "How should I respond?" and the word response.

Summary Points from Rescued
Part 4: Response

Asking God for the graces of gratitude, surrender and courage.

Key Truths

- In response to His rescue, Jesus invites us to both an internal and an external mission.

- Our internal response to Jesus is worship and thanksgiving (the Mass), complete surrender, and personal sanctity.

- We need to know from personal experience that Christ is the answer to every human ill, the solution to every human problem. We need to know and understand The Story so that we can share it.

- We start our mission in our own sphere of influence (marriage, friendships, profession).

- Our external response is more expansive: He's calling us rescue others and become agents of sabotage.

- ⚜ God is the one leading us as we try to help Him get His world back.

- ⚜ The Holy Spirit enables me to do all of this.

- ⚜ The Mission? To help God get his world back, "So that in Jesus Christ, all might be rescued, and have abundant life, for the glory of the Father." (cf. John 10:10)

*Optional: lead a prayer of surrender
(below) to Jesus at the end of the homily.*

Prayer for Surrender

God, I believe that out of Your infinite love, You created me. I'm sorry for all the times I have believed the enemy's lies that You are not a good Father and that You don't love me. Please forgive me for all of my sins. Thank You for sending Jesus, the Ambush Predator, to rescue me from sin, death, hell and Satan. I choose this day to place Your Son, Jesus, at the center of my life.

And so, today, here and now, I surrender to You, Jesus, and desire Your lordship over every area of my life. I ask You now to flood my soul with the gift of the Holy Spirit. Help me to know my true identity as a beloved son/daughter. Help me to know that I matter and that I am worth dying for. Recreate me to be the person You destined me to be. Please use me as an instrument in your merciful hands to rescue others and to help recreate this world that You so love. Amen.

Consider

Focusing on a personal response to the kerygma raises the question for each individual, "If God has done all of this for me, and for the world, how should I respond to those acts of love?" The response is two-fold: holiness, beginning with a complete surrender of one's life to God, and mission. We are invited to surrender our lives to God anew, or possibly for some, for the first time. Prayerfully consider leading the congregations in a prayer of surrender (see above example) at the end of the homily if they wish to respond. Special consideration should be given to how the liturgy is an act of response. How do we respond? "Take this, all of you, and eat of it."

There is also a mission response. If this good news is meant for everyone to have an opportunity to respond, how should my love of neighbor compel me to be a part of God's plan for rescuing others? If some were still lost in captivity, how would that compel me, in love, to go to others with this news?

Possible Verses for Focus

Isaiah 7:14 – "Therefore the Lord himself will give you this sign: the virgin shall conceive, and bear a son, and shall name him Emmanuel." God's desire to save us from sin leads to him working outside of the natural order, bringing life to the womb of a virgin to avoid the damages of original sin. In this act, he defies the "victory" of Satan over humanity.

Romans 1:4 – "...established as Son of God in power according to the Spirit of holiness through resurrection from the dead, Jesus Christ our Lord." Christ is not just Lord because he's God Creator of all things, but because he has overcome Satan's evil destruction of humanity. In freeing us from sin, God has given us back the gift of free will. As created, we are free to choose him. "Through him we have received the grace of apostleship, to bring about the obedience of faith" (v.5) In his overwhelming mercy, God sent His Son to establish right ordered love in relationships giving us the choice of grace in following Christ. We are each given the opportunity to choose God for ourselves, instead of continuing to suffer under the yoke of original sin.

Matthew 1:20–21 – "For it is through the Holy Spirit that this child has been conceived in her. She will bear a son and you are to name him Jesus, because he will save his people from their sins." Through the brokenness of humanity, God (who is love) chooses to redeem a sinful people held captive by their pride. God's infinite desire to know each of us personally is only possible by restoring our will to choose a relationship with him. More than anything, he desires to intimately live with us; through all the trials of life to offer hope and peace and joy. This is clearly reflected in the ultimate gift he shares–his son–"and they shall name him Emmanuel, which means 'God is with us.'(v.23) Through his son, God offers each of us – in every moment – the ongoing invitation to be with him.

Monday, December 22

1 Samuel 1:24-28; Luke 1:46-56

"He remembered his promise of mercy"

We tend to have a very limited idea of mercy. We think mercy only comes about because we sin, and so when God doesn't give us the punishment we deserve for our sins, He is having mercy on us. But that's not the biblical understanding of mercy; in Scripture, and here in the Magnificat, mercy speaks more about God Himself than it does about us.

The word used here in Luke is eleos, the Greek word equivalent of the Hebrew chesed: both speak about God's faithfulness to himself, to His fidelity to His covenantal love with us, to His fidelity to His nature as merciful to all he has created. In English, these words get translated as "steadfast love," "loving kindness," "mercy," "faithfulness," each translation showing an aspect of what we mean when we say God is merciful.

Mercy isn't simply a lack of punishment when we sin. It is God being God toward us, that is God being faithful, patient, loving, steadfast, always and in every situation. That's why the Psalms, for example, are filled with requests for God to be merciful; they're saying, "God, show us that you are still God!"

And no matter how many times the people of Israel turned their back on God, no matter how many times they broke the covenant, no matter how many times they were unfaithful to him, they could still pray for him to be merciful and pray with absolute confidence, because God is faithful to Himself, to his own nature of loving tenderly and steadfastly those whom He has created in His own image.

That same promise of mercy is a promise for each of our lives, too: God will be faithful to His covenant with us, to the covenant He sealed in His own blood on the cross, to the covenant to love us and heal us and rescue us. He remembers his promise of mercy in each of our lives. So whatever you are facing today, you can pray, "Lord God, remember Your mercy. Show Yourself, reveal Yourself, in this situation, faithful and loving God."

Questions for reflection

1. How have I tended to think of God's mercy? Does hearing that it means his faithfulness to his nature as loving and steadfast change anything for me?

2. When have I experienced the steadfastness of God's love for me?

3. What can I do today to live with greater trust in God's mercy?

Action

Present to the Lord any situation in which you need Him to reveal his faithful and steadfast love to you, then throughout the day, look for the signs of His mercy and write them down at the end of the day.

Tuesday, December 23

MALACHI 3:1–4, 23–24; LUKE 1:57–66

"Immediately his mouth was opened"

When the angel Gabriel first came to Zechariah to tell him that he and Elizabeth would have a child, Zechariah doubted, wanting proof of the angel's message, not believing that it was possible. And this left him in a time of trial, unable to speak, needing to depend on others to help him communicate, and the silence must have given him much time to meditate on the message of the angel and the visit of Mary, pregnant with the Messiah, on her prompt and wholehearted response.

This time in silence, in fact, in silence before the miracle of his own son's conception, before the miracle of Mary's conception of the Messiah and her presence in his own home, has transformed something in him. He knows now that the fitting response to God isn't to ask for proof of his messages or for an explanation of all the details. Rather, the fitting response to God is obedience, is to listen with his whole being and welcome the word of God, and then act on whatever it is God has said.

So when they hand him the tablet, he is ready. He has no expectations that obedience will bring his speech back to him. He simply knows that he must obey, and that obeying is the only thing he really wants to do. So he takes the tablet and writes, "John is his name," and everyone is amazed that he wants to name his son John. But then something more amazing happens: suddenly, Zechariah, who has been mute for more than nine months, can speak again.

Obedience to the Lord brings freedom. Whereas sin, disobedience, brings captivity and bondage, obedience always brings freedom. In Zechariah's case, it freed him to speak again, and freed his speech to be full of praise and blessing, not of worry and trying to control. And the impact of his obedience went far beyond himself. It touched each of the people there who heard him speak again, and spread throughout his whole neighborhood.

When we obey, we are set free. And when we obey, we touch others' lives in ways we could never have imagined. So the next time you are faced with a decision to obey God or to do your own will, think about the freedom that will spread from your obedience, through your own life, and through the lives of all you touch.

Questions for reflection

1. When have you obeyed God and found greater freedom? How did this happen?

2. What do you usually think of when you hear the word "obey"? Why?

3. Where is it most difficult in your life to surrender your own will to the will of the Father?

Action

Make a list of those in your life whom you most want to see rescued by the Lord, and when you struggle to do the will of God, think of how your obedience is part of their rescue.

Wednesday, December 24

2 Samuel 7:1–5, 8b–12, 14a, 16; Luke 1:67–79

"Blessed be the Lord"

The last night of my first foreign mission trip, the priest guiding it suggested that we spend part of the time in our holy hour writing down all the blessings from the trip. We were doing nocturnal adoration, getting up in the middle of the night to adore the Lord, and I remember that I stayed in that little chapel in Mexico for two and a half hours, writing down blessings, and when that time was over, I still wasn't halfway through the first week. I went back to the school where we were staying, but couldn't sleep, not when there were so many blessings still to count. So I stayed up, watching the sunrise over the desert, writing blessing after blessing in my spiritual journal. And by the time the rest of the group was up in the morning, I was beginning to rush, and had maybe finished the blessings of the first week. After Mass, I went up to the priest and told him it was an impossible assignment, and that it had made me realize that, were I to really count all of my blessings, I would never do anything else.

But so much of the time I forget to count my blessings, and I think that's probably true for many of us. Maybe we tend toward scrupulosity and spend the whole of our examination of conscience at the end of the day agonizingly looking for our sins. Or maybe we tend to have a negative outlook on life and are hyper–focused on the things that go wrong or could go wrong. Or maybe we are simply distracted, caught up in busy–ness or wasting time on social media, and we simply fail to notice all the blessings.

What Zechariah reminds us to do is to pay attention and to bless the Lord for all the many blessings He has given us.

We don't have to wait until the end of an important experience. We don't have to wait until the end of the day. We can praise Him in the moment. We can live with an attitude of gratitude, with eyes wide open to the wonders of the Lord, to the many ways He blesses us each day.

And when we do, when we live with grateful hearts, hearts lifted up always in praise and blessing, we will find that we grow ever more aware of God's blessings, in our own lives and in the lives of those around us. So let's decide today to count our blessings, whatever our crosses, and know that the blessings always outnumber the challenges, the gifts of God are always more abundant than our sins.

Questions for reflection

1. How attuned is your heart to the ways that God is blessing you? What can you do to make it more attentive to His blessings?

2. What have been the greatest blessings of God in your life thus far?

3. What are the daily blessings that you, in general, don't even pay attention to? What gets in the way of your noticing them?

Action
Today, spend at least ten minutes counting your blessings just of today, and then praise and bless God for His goodness to you.

Thursday, December 25

CHRISTMAS DAY

Isaiah 62:11–12; Titus 3:4–7; Luke 2:15–20

"Mary kept all these things, reflecting on them in her heart"

Our culture, I think, tends toward activism. We always want to be doing something, to feel productive, to have something to show for our time. We want to make a difference, want to leave a mark. And that can be true for us as followers of Jesus, too—we want to see results from following Him, want to be able to quantify, somehow, our fruitfulness.

Mary, as always, wants to show us a better way. Here she is in the center of the scene, holding the baby Jesus in her arms, peacefully and quietly adoring him in the humble cave where He was born, surrounded by the animals, the smell of warm straw in the cold winter air. And in come the shepherds and excitedly tell her and Joseph about the hosts of angels singing and praising God and the message of the angel, and right there before her, the shepherds are being saved by the child she holds in her arms, and certainly her heart is filled with wonder and awe.

But she doesn't run off to be productive, doesn't try to calculate the fruits of her yes, doesn't busy herself to get more things done. No, she stays, adoring her Son, pondering in her heart all that has happened, not just in her own life in the last nine months, but in the history of her people.

She doesn't let any work of the Lord slip through her hands. She doesn't let anything about his presence pass her by. She keeps in her heart everything He has done and everything He is doing, going over it again and again, pondering it, seeking to understand it, and loving ever more He who has done it.

Mary teaches us that, for as much as the work of rescue requires us to act, it also requires us to be still and to know that God is God, to savor the things He has done, to treasure in our hearts His presence and His action, to let them expand and express their full meaning over time.

Today, Christmas Day, let's imitate Mary. Let's spend some time pondering in our hearts all that Jesus' birth in this world has meant for our own lives. Let's not let ourselves lose sight of this great mystery by the many elements of the celebration, but find some quiet to let the meaning unfold within us.

Questions for reflection

1. How much time do you tend to spend pondering the works of the Lord, holding them in your heart?

2. In what ways do you tend to activism? How does the Lord invite you to adopt a more Marian, more contemplative attitude in those areas of your life?

3. What actions of the Lord in your life have you kept and pondered in your hearts? How has the meaning of these actions become fuller as you ponder them?

Action

At the end of the day today, spend 10 minutes in quiet contemplation of the baby Jesus in the nativity scene, thinking of the impact of His birth in your own life.

Friday, December 26

SAINT STEPHEN

ACTS 6:8–10, 7:54–59; MATTHEW 10:17–22

"Lord, do not hold this sin against them"

In how St. Stephen dies, we see that his whole life was configured to the life of Jesus Christ. Like Jesus, he is unjustly accused and condemned to die. Like Jesus, he accepts that death. Like Jesus, in one of the last actions of his life, he chooses to forgive those who are stoning him to death, and prays for God to forgive them.

Forgiveness is one of the greatest acts of sabotage that we have as agents of transformation. Nothing so derails Satan's designs as forgiveness. No other act that is within our power, I think, has the power of forgiveness.

What makes forgiveness so powerful? How does forgiveness sabotage the Enemy's strategies?

When others hurt us, we naturally want to shield our hearts from them, to protect ourselves from being hurt again. Resentment, anger, bitterness, those things are like barriers between us and that person—but without our ever intending it, are also barriers between us and God, because if we harden our hearts to others, we harden our hearts to God. So in the first place, forgiveness sabotages the work of the Enemy in our own hearts—it frees us from resentment and bitterness and makes our hearts soft and open to the grace of God.

But it doesn't just transform our own hearts. Forgiveness has the power to set the other person free, to open their heart to God's grace, to open to them a path of reconciliation and new life. When we forgive others, we give them the chance, through us, of experiencing God's mercy. It is incredibly powerful, restoring relationships, healing wounds, bringing new life.

And we see that in St. Stephen. Because Saul was listening to his prayer that God forgive, and later on experienced himself the fruits of that prayer, and Saul became St. Paul.

Nothing undermines Satan's work in our lives so powerfully as forgiveness. And nothing unlocks for our own hearts more powerfully the fullness of God's work of redemption. Today let's decide to blow up Satan's plans, remembering that our only enemy is the Enemy, and let's become agents of sabotage and agents of transformation for all those who have hurt us by forgiving them from our hearts and praying for them to experience God's forgiveness.

Questions for reflection

1. When have you experienced the power of forgiving another person? What changed in your own heart?

2. Have you witnessed the power of forgiveness to change others' lives? How and when?

3. Who do you need to forgive today?

Action

For each person or offense that you need to forgive, draw a bomb and write that person/action on it, then throw them into a fire, and imagine visually what it looks like to sabotage Satan's strategy in your own life and in the life of each of the persons you are forgiving.

Saturday, December 27

SAINT JOHN THE EVANGELIST

1 John 1:1–4; John 20:1a and 2–8

"What we have seen and heard we proclaim now to you"

There's a lovely scene in one of the episodes of The Chosen, when Jesus is speaking with the woman at the well in Samaria. When she believes that he really is the Messiah, she says, "I'm going to tell everyone!" And Jesus responds to her, "I was counting on it." Like St. John, she feels the need to proclaim all that Jesus has said and done for her, all that she has seen and heard. And her testimony is so powerful, Scripture tells us, that many of the people of the town come to see Jesus for themselves and then believe in Him.

The woman at the well didn't have any special training. She wasn't in a position of prestige or authority. She didn't have great financial resources. She wasn't even accepted in her community.

But she had encountered Jesus, she had come to believe in Him, and she knew that everyone needed to know Him, everyone needed to encounter Him as she had. So she ran and began to tell everyone she knew, even everyone she saw, that she had found the Messiah, and she was so convinced of her testimony and so convincing in relating her testimony that many came to believe because of her. She had been rescued, and she ran back to those in captivity to tell them they could be rescued, too.

That's all it takes, really, to bring people to Jesus. We don't need much more than the story of our personal encounter with Him: how we met Him, what He told us and did for us, how our life has changed because of knowing Him. If you've met Jesus, if He's really transformed your life, you simply can't keep it to yourself. You have to tell others, because they need to know.

You don't need to be a trained theologian. You don't need to be a polished public speaker. You don't need to know or proclaim more than what you have seen and heard. All you need to know is who Jesus is and what He has done for you.

When you proclaim that, convinced that Jesus is who He says He is, convinced that Jesus is the One who has rescued you and transformed your life, then, like the woman at the well, like St. John, and like whoever it was who first told you about Jesus, your testimony will have the power of conviction and you will bring others to him. And just like Jesus was counting on the woman at the well, he is counting on you. Bring them to Him, and He will do the rest.

Questions for reflection

1. How did you first meet Jesus? How did that encounter change your life?

2. What are the things you have seen and heard Jesus do and say? What is the message you have to proclaim?

3. With whom is the Lord calling you to share your testimony?

Action
Today, tell someone you know the story of how you met Jesus and what He has done in your life.

Sunday, December 28

HOLY FAMILY

Sirach 3:2–6, 12–14;
Colossians 3:12–21 or 3:12–17;
Matthew 2:13–15, 19–23

"Take the child and his mother"

There is often a great temptation in life to compartmentalize, a tendency toward a lack of unity. Often, and especially early on when we decide to follow Jesus, we can live our life of faith as if it were one sector of our lives, not something all-encompassing, something that penetrates and permeates our whole being and thus every sphere of our lives: family, friendships, school or work, aspirations, goals, projects, church, hobbies, everything.

Joseph doesn't compartmentalize. The message he receives—and that we all receive—is to take the child and his mother—Jesus and Mary—with us wherever we go. He receives the message and he acts on it: he takes the child and his mother to Egypt, takes them back again to Israel. He has made Jesus the center of his life, and intentionally brings Him everywhere with him.

Jesus hasn't rescued us just so we don't live in slavery; He's rescued us so that we know the joy and fullness of life that comes from living in his presence, from receiving the new life He brings into every aspect of our life, letting his grace and His presence transform our relationship with family, with friends, our work, our studies, our goals and plans, our hobbies. He wants us to live life to the fullest, and He knows that the fullness of life is something we can only receive from Him.

Taking the child and His mother with us into every area of our lives can be challenging, because it can mean changes. For sure it means we have to be intentional in our choices, in our words, in our actions. It's enough to think about one of the areas where we tend to ignore His presence or intentionally leave Him behind to recognize what we would have to change if we were to bring Him along.

But we don't have to be afraid of those changes. Instead, we can, like Joseph, simply trust. My life is now bound up with the life of Jesus, so wherever He leads I will go, and I will let Him into every aspect of my life. He didn't enter my life to stay in the ADU or guest room, but to be Lord of the entire house. So today, let's choose to be like Joseph and take Jesus into every aspect of our lives and let His presence transform us.

Questions for reflection

1. Are there any areas of your life into which you haven't yet welcomed Jesus? What ones?

2. What difference has welcoming Jesus into your life made? What differences does He still want to make?

3. Is there anything you are afraid that Jesus might change if you welcome Him more fully? Why?

Action

Take a small baby Jesus figurine or a crucifix with you today wherever you go, and put Him always in a place where you can see Him.

Monday, December 29

1 John 2:3-11; Luke 2:22-35

"He took him into his arms and blessed God"

One of the dangers of the mysteries of our faith is that we can get used to them. We can get used to the astonishing fact that the Creator of all that exists was born in a specific moment of history, that He was seen and touched and loved and fed by real historical persons. And we can wonder at the mystery of it all: eternal and almighty God as an infant in His mother's arms, wearing a diaper and wrapped in swaddling clothes.

Why did God do this? Why did He come as a baby, so helpless and defenseless and dependent on others? Why did He make Himself so vulnerable to our love or our rejection? Why did He make Himself so easy to pick up or put down?

I think we see the answer in this moment of his presentation in the temple. Scripture says that Simeon took the infant Jesus in his arms. Simeon, who had waited for this moment for his whole long life, now can receive Jesus, can embrace God, can look at the face of God and live, can welcome with a full embrace, all that God is and all that God wants to do in his life.

God could simply overwhelm us with His love. He could overpower us. He could constantly make us feel our tininess, our otherness, our distance from him. But instead, He comes in tenderness and smallness, makes Himself one of us, comes as a baby so that we can receive Him and embrace Him.

That's how His salvation tends to come into our lives, too: small offers, little steps, things we can accept and embrace and allow to become part of us without overwhelming us. All we have to do is receive each offer of salvation as it comes.

And that should give us great hope, too, for those for whom we are praying: just as God came as a tiny baby to Simeon so that Simeon could embrace Him, just as the Lord offers us salvation step by step, in ways small enough for us to receive without overpowering us, so, too, is He at work in the hearts of those dear to us, gradually allowing Himself to be accepted, received, and embraced by them.

Questions for reflection

1. When you look back at your life this past year, in what ways do you see that the Lord has been manifesting His salvation little by little, so that you could receive and embrace His action in your life?

2. If you look at the lives of those for whom you are praying, can you see small signs that the Lord is at work in them? What are those signs?

3. What would have been lost in your own humanity (maybe your sense of freedom or personal agency or sense of identity) if, rather than working slowly in you, step by step, in small ways, God had overpowered you with healing or conversion?

Action

For each of the things you prayed in the above questions, imagine that you are Simeon, and that each one of those things or actions of God in your life is Jesus coming to you as a baby, and choose to receive and embrace Him and that work in your life a plan for how you will cooperate with this work of rescue.

Tuesday, December 30

1 John 2:12–17; Luke 2:36–40

"She gave thanks to God and spoke about the child to all..."

Let's start with a thought experiment. Take out a sheet of paper and write down everyone you know. Then, next to those whom you know who are already Christians, draw a small cross. Next to those whom you know that you know also know other Christians, draw a horizontal arrow going outward. Next to those whom you know but don't know if they know any other Christians, write an asterisk.

How many are they? How many people do you know who don't know Jesus, and who not only don't know Him, but don't know someone else who does?

The prophetess Anna encountered Jesus in the Temple that day when Mary and Joseph brought in their infant Son. And immediately, she began to speak of Him to all those who hadn't seen Him or didn't know Him as she did. There was no delay. Why? Because she knew that Jesus was for everyone, that this Child was meant to save everyone, not just some, not just her, not just those who happened to be there at that precise moment.

The same is true in your life and in mine. The Child in His mother's arms is not just for us. He's for everyone. That rescue you've experienced, it's not just for you, it's for all your fellow captives, who are probably now wondering where you are and what has happened to you.

There are so many people suffering so badly simply because they don't know Jesus. There are so many people trapped in the Enemy's bunkers because no one has spoken to them about the child. There are so many people hopelessly confused by lies because no one has introduced them to the Truth.

And that's where you and I come in. Those people on your list and on mine, the ones who don't know any other Christians, how can they know if you and I don't tell them? Who will tell them if we don't?

The thought experiment has to be transformed from a list on paper to a specific mission. You are meant to be the agent of rescue in their lives. You are the one who can proclaim the good news to them. You are the one who can speak about Jesus to them. You are the one who can bring them to Him.

Do you think God didn't know you knew them? Do you think that you are not part of His strategy for their rescue? So what are you waiting for?

Questions for reflection

1. What keeps you from speaking about the work that the Lord has done in your life with those who don't know Him?

2. What will it take for the asterisks on your list to be transformed into crosses?

Action

Next to each person on your list whom you marked with an asterisk, write down a concrete plan for sharing Jesus with them.

Wednesday, December 31

1 John 2:18–21; John 1:1–18

"He gave them power to become children of God"

It's easy to feel powerless when we look at the world we live in. We vote for life, for example, but then the awful bill promoting abortions passes anyway. We read the news, and the world seems like it's spinning out of control with wars and famines, crimes and addictions. We drive through our city streets and see the way Satan is destroying lives through powerful addictions. What can we do? We are so small, and the evil in the world seems so big, so daunting, so powerful.

St. John writes that to those who believe in Jesus, He gives the power to become children of God. The power to become children of God. The power to live like Jesus. The power to act like Jesus. The power to pray like Jesus.

Jesus promises this power in the Great Commission. He tells us that in His name we will drive out demons, speak new languages, lay hands on the sick and heal them, and not be harmed by evil.

We're the ones who don't believe that we have this power. We forget that the power of God lives in us, that the Holy Spirit has been poured into our hearts, that we have the power to be and to live and to act as children of God, that Jesus is with us always, that whatever we ask the Father in His name we will receive.

Maybe I can't do something to solve the problem of fentanyl on the streets of my city. But I can do something to overthrow the Enemy's power in the life of one person suffering from addiction. I can go to him, meet him, listen to his story, share the love of Jesus with him, and pray in faith for him. And I can go back again and again and again, as long as it takes, not giving in to the temptation to discouragement. Not because I can do anything on my own, but because in Christ, I have the power to live as child of God, because in Christ I am empowered by the Holy Spirit to do what Jesus would do.

And you can fight whatever battle it is He is calling you to fight for whatever soul He has entrusted to you. Not because you are strong or powerful on your own, but because in Christ you have the power of the Holy Spirit to participate in the work of rescue.

Jesus promised us that the gates of hell will not prevail against us. He promised us that He will be with us always. He commanded us to go into all the world and proclaim the Gospel. He is not afraid. He is not withdrawing His hand from us. He is not retreating. He has poured his Holy Spirit into our hearts. And He is waiting for us to clothe ourselves in the full armor of God, pick up our swords, and go to battle.

Questions for reflection

1. When you look at the situations of evil today, where do you experience that the Lord is calling you to fight?

2. What is the difference that Jesus is asking you to make? In the life of whom?

3. What keeps you from living with more power, praying with more power, acting with more power?

4. How would your mission look different if you believed you have the power to be a child of God?

> ### Action
>
> Ask the Holy Spirit to anoint you anew for your mission and to increase your faith in His power at work in you and through you. Stay in this prayer until you experience that you have received a new anointing from on high.

Thursday, January 1

MARY MOTHER OF GOD

NUMBERS 6:22–27; GALATIANS 4:4–7; LUKE 2:16–21

"You are no longer a slave but a child"

As often happens when people become afraid in relationships, those to whom we minister on the streets can sometimes try to push us away. They don't do it by trying to scare us or by threatening us. They do it by putting themselves down, by trying to prove to themselves through us their own worthlessness. It happened recently with Thomas, a man whom I have known for several years and who has become very dear to me. Basically, he said, "I don't know why you bother, Sister."

I responded: "Because you're worth it."

"I'm a meth addict" he replied.

"No, you're not."

"I use a lot of meth."

"Okay, but that doesn't define you. That's not who you are."

"I'm a convicted violent felon."

"No, you're not."

He then told me what he's been convicted of, to which I responded, "You may have done that, but that doesn't define you, that's not who you are."

He didn't quite know what to say, but looked at me, lost, confused. So I said, "Thomas, look me in the eyes. You know who you are? You are a beloved child of God and you are my friend and I love you. That's who you are." Tears filled his eyes. I don't think he'd ever heard that before.

It didn't miraculously end his addiction or move him into housing or lead him to the sacraments. But it did something in his heart and mine. For the first time, he has open to him the possibility, the hope, that he can be a beloved child of God, this man who was never treated as beloved by his parents. And as I spoke those words to him, I became more convinced both of their truth for him and for me.

"We are not," St. John Paul II said, "the sum of our weaknesses and failures. We are the sum of the Father's love for us and our real capacity to become the image of His Son Jesus."

If you are reading this, it's because you have been rescued, because you know—at least in part—that you are a beloved child of God, because you have been growing in that identity and in the inner security that you are a child of God. That means that you must daily cast off the false claims that still speak in your heart, the claims of slavery, and live more and more fully into that identity.

And telling others who they really are, beloved sons and daughters of an eternally loving Father, is both a fruit of that new identity and a way of deepening that identity. There are people like my friend Thomas everywhere, housed and unhoused, who don't know that they are children of God. This new year, let's make it our resolution to tell them who they really are and to do everything in our power to bring them into the Father's house.

Questions for reflection

1. What is one lie from the Enemy you can resolve to renounce in this new year, so that you can live more fully as a child of God?

2. In what ways have you grown in your identity as a child of God? How has knowing this is your true identity changed you?

3. Who in your life doesn't know he or she is a beloved child of God? What can you do to both show and tell that person his or her true identity?

Action

Write the phrase, "I am no longer a slave, but a child of God" in a place where you can see it every day this year.

About *"Hail Full of Grace"*
ADELE PIERCE

I wrote the icon, *"Hail Full of Grace"* between September of 2022 and March of 2023. Without a doubt, this creative act was a prayer entirely inspired by the Holy Spirit.

In it, Mary, a young girl, faces us, her gaze inviting, strong and completely confident. She is seen in a grand scale to symbolize that who she is cannot be contained within the canvas. Her golden halo, immense and decorated with juniper branches and a portion of the Hail Mary prayer in Latin, is intended to draw our attention so that we are compelled to remain in the image, traveling around it with our eyes and responding to her gentle invitation to love.

To read more about *"Hail Full of Grace"* please visit:
lorrainecross.media/adele

About the Author
SR. TERESA HARRELL

Sr. Teresa Harrell is a member of the Society of Mary, religious missionary Sisters dedicated to the New Evangelization who work with the Saint John Society in their programs of New Evangelization. While in graduate school at Oregon State, she encountered Jesus alive in the Eucharist and entered the Church in 2002. She is currently serving at St. Michael the Archangel in downtown Portland, Oregon, where (among other things) she directs Mercy Mission program. She completed undergraduate studies in English and philosophy, Master's degrees in English and Theology, and is currently working on a D.Min.

About the Creator of The Rescue Project
FR. JOHN RICCARDO

Fr. John Riccardo is a priest, author, syndicated radio host, and Executive Director of ACTS XXIX. Ordained for the Archdiocese of Detroit in 1996, he has degrees from the University of Michigan, the Gregorian University in Rome, and the Pope John Paul II Institute for Studies on Marriage and the Family in Washington, DC. He's authored numerous books including *Rescued*; *Heaven Starts Now*; *Rerouting*; *Learning to Trust from Mary* and *Unshakable Hope*. After more than twenty years in parish ministry, Fr. John founded ACTS XXIX, an international non–profit Catholic apostolate whose mission is to renew and transform the Church by unleashing the power of the gospel, equipping ordained and lay leaders in order to mobilize the Church for mission. Launched by ACTS XXIX in 2022, *The Rescue Project* is a global movement that proclaims the gospel in a compelling and attractive way. The experience creates an opportunity for people to be overwhelmed by the gospel, brought to a decision to surrender their lives to Jesus, and mobilized for mission. The series is being offered across the United States and in over 30 countries around the world.

About ACTS XXIX and The Rescue Project

ACTS XXIX is a non–profit, international Catholic apostolate founded in 2019 by Fr. John Riccardo. ACTS XXIX unleashes the power of the gospel and equips ordained and lay leaders with the three essential principles for transformation in order to mobilize the Church for mission. These principles are incarnated in four missions: *The Rescue Project,* Immersive Leadership Team Experiences, Revive and Equip Clergy and Seminarians, Media and Events. Please visit **actsxxix.org** for more information.

Launched by ACTS XXIX in 2022, *The Rescue Project* is a global movement that proclaims the gospel in a compelling and attractive way. Available for free and in multiple languages, *The Rescue Project* aims to provide people with an opportunity to be overwhelmed by what God has done for us, surrender their lives to Him and get mobilized for mission.

The eight–week video experience of *The Rescue Project* is intended for use anywhere–in parish ministries such as OCIA, sacramental preparation, evangelization, discipleship, men's groups, women's groups, youth ministry, and more. It can also be run in homes, restaurants, workplaces, seminaries, universities, and prisons. *The Rescue Project* appeals to those who have been walking with Jesus for years, as well as to others for whom Jesus is only a figure in ancient history. In other words, *The Rescue Project* is for everyone, everywhere, whether inside or outside the Church. All the resources needed to run *The Rescue Project* are available online free–of–charge at **rescueproject.us**

✝ lorraine
cross *media*

A MISSION OF ACTS XXIX

Creating media that inspires, encourages and breathes hope.

Lorraine Cross Media, a mission of ACTS XXIX, produces and distributes books, film, and various online content. To learn more please visit **lorrainecross.media/about**